D0350401

The Complete Guide to

WRITING BIOGRAPHIES

The Complete Guide to

WRITING BIOGRAPHIES

Ted Schwarz

Writer's Digest Books

Cincinnati, Ohio

The Complete Guide to Writing Biographies. Copyright © 1990 by Ted Schwarz. Printed and bound in the United States of America. All rights reserved. No part of this book may be reproduced in any form or by any electronic or mechanical means including information storage and retrieval systems without permission in writing from the publisher, except by a reviewer, who may quote brief passages in a review. Published by Writer's Digest Books, an imprint of F&W Publications, Inc., 1507 Dana Ave., Cincinnati, Ohio 45207. First edition.

94 93 92 91 90   5 4 3 2 1

Library of Congress Cataloging-in-Publication Data

Schwarz, Ted
  The complete guide to writing biographies / Ted Schwarz.
    p.   cm.
  ISBN 0-89879-407-2
  1. Biography (as a literary form) 2. Authorship. I. Title.
CT21.S38 1990   90-12149
808'.06692 — dc20   CIP

*To Leslie, who taught me to be vulnerable
so I could tell the story of others.*

About the Author

Ted Schwarz is the author, co-author, or "ghost" of more than sixty books and 2,000 articles. His first as-told-to autobiography, *The Five of Me* (with Henry Hawksworth), became a CBS Movie of the Week starring David Birney. Since then his work has been used for international documentaries (*The Hillside Strangler*), been on international best seller lists (*DeLorean* with John DeLorean; *The Peter Lawford Story* with Patricia S. Lawford; etc.), and provided an insider's look at labor unions and politics (*Power and Greed: Inside the Teamsters Empire of Corruption* with Allen Friedman). He has worked with major celebrities and written historical biographies such as his forthcoming *Walking with the Damned: The Folke Bernadotte Story*.

CONTENTS

The Complete Guide to

WRITING BIOGRAPHIES

INTRODUCTION

For thousands of years, humans have been interested in both sharing the stories of their own lives and reading about the lives of others. It might be said that the earliest autobiographies were the drawings on walls produced by prehistoric man. A wandering stranger offered the hospitality of a cave might find the retelling of an adventure that brought Og, the Neanderthal, to a fight to the death against a woolly mammoth.

Later, heroic exploits were related in drawings on the sides of vases and urns. The ancient Romans often used their coins to tell of leadership changes, wars won, and construction projects completed by their emperors. At times, even sex scandals, such as the story of Nero and his mother, Agrippina, could be understood through the coinage. Whether the portrait heads of leaders were shown equally on the obverse, one head was shown more prominently than the other, or one head was on the obverse, the other on the reverse, all spoke of power plays to illiterate citizens who studied their coinage in the manner that we read gossip magazines. A handful of pocket change helped illiterate citizens in the far-flung corners of the Empire hear stories that were the equivalent, for the time, of the modern autobiographies of men such as New York–based developer Donald Trump.

Over the centuries people became more literate. Biography was recorded on scrolls, many of the records relating to both government and religious leaders. The Bible, in part, can be considered a collective biography. Then there were the biographers of men and women of letters, such as James Boswell's life of Sam Johnson. In 1795, the Duke of Dorset's collection of historic portraits was discussed in a collective biography relating the stories behind the men shown. In 1800, collective biographies of statesmen and writers became popular. Writers such as Abraham Hayward, James Bruce, George Robert Glieg, Charles Seymour, and others were quite popular for their collective biographies, an approach that dated back to Plutarchus, the author of *Plutarch's Lives* written several centuries earlier.

Generally the subjects were men and women involved with politics, religion, or business. By the early 1900s, collective biographies often glorified the lives of the poor who were able to rise to great wealth. The ideal image was the person who had pulled him- or herself "up by the boot straps."

Today the biography and as-told-to autobiography have become the most popular sources of nonfiction reading in the United

States, a situation publishers do not expect to change in the years ahead. Whether a triumph over adversity, the story of the formerly mighty who have met a tragic fate, or the inside story of a type of life few of us could ever imagine living, such books are regularly on the best seller lists. First printings are frequently five to ten times the numbers of other nonfiction categories. And because the subject, not the author, is what is important to the public, even a first-time writer can score a major success.

Fascination with the biography and as-told-to autobiography has extended beyond just the book-buying public. Magazines such as *People, Us, Vanity Fair, Spy,* the *National Enquirer*, and numerous others are eagerly awaited by millions of readers every month. Sometimes their profiles are excerpts from a major book. Other times the people they profile will soon be the subject of one or more volumes eagerly awaited in the bookstores. Whatever the case, this is a category for which men and women, both in the United States and abroad, have an avid, seemingly insatiable appetite.

This field is not for adults only, however. Biographies written for children are increasingly popular in an age where heroes are not likely to be found on the front pages of the daily paper. Religious publishers seek books on both the humble and the famous who have triumphed in the face of almost overwhelming circumstances. Secular publishers want the stories of the greats in politics, sports, social achievement, and related areas.

And both juvenile and adult publishers seek works on historic individuals whose lives must be traced through extensive study in archives, newspaper files, historical society holdings, and similar locations. The passions, triumphs, and failures of individuals are just as exciting whether they happened last year or last century. In fact, they are sometimes easier to sell because they can be pegged around a special event — an anniversary, a literary or artistic retrospective, or something similar.

The biography or as-told-to autobiography has a power greater than its impact in the marketplace. Well researched and accurately presented, such books have changed the course of history. Books such as Nan Britten's *The President's Daughter*, Carl Bernstein and Bob Woodward's books such as *All the President's Men* and *The Final Days* have proven the downfall of political leaders. Criminals, frauds, and corruption in government have been exposed in such volumes as Thomas Thompson's *Blood and Money*, Joe McGinnis' *Fatal Vision*, Thomas Renner's as-told-to *My Life in the Mafia* by Vincent Teresa, and numerous others. They have righted wrongs, revealed hidden truths that have altered the course of history, and otherwise had a disproportionate impact on the society at large. If it is true that the pen is mightier than the sword, then the biography may be the pen at its most powerful.

Naturally such a weapon must be used with care. There are libel concerns to be addressed, moral and ethical issues to be considered. Yet once addressed, such issues only help to focus such books, to make them stronger, more fascinating, with greater potential impact.

ONE

Why a Biography?

I frequently tell students in writing classes that writers have the best jobs in the world. We are paid to be nosey. And nowhere is this more a reality than with a biography or an as-told-to autobiography.

The story of an individual is probably the most complex story you will ever write. We tend to see individuals only under the best or worst of circumstances when we first learn about them. Adolf Hitler wants to start the Third Reich and determines that millions will die while he establishes his master race. Martin Luther King, Jr., recognizes that the arrest of Rosa Parks, too tired and too fed up with racial bigotry to move to the back of a mostly empty bus, is an outrage. He organizes the Montgomery, Alabama, bus boycott and changes the course of American history for decades. Lise Meitner becomes curious about Einstein's theories, discovers how to split the atom, and makes the atomic age a reality.

These are all facts of history. One person is evil. A second is heroic. A third is brilliant. We use simple adjectives to briefly honor or abhor the individual, then get on with more interesting concerns.

But the biographer recognizes that there is more to figures of history than notoriety. Each man and woman is complex, passionate, capable of a wide range of actions and emotions. The people and forces at work in their lives, from birth through death, shape them, give them their bias, affect their subconscious, and drive them in ways that are often far more fascinating than just the surface.

Hitler was a lover of animals and children, provided they were a part of what he perceived to be the basis for his master race. He had hot cocoa parties for the children in the family of Joseph Goebbels, his propaganda minister. He made Magda Goebbels the first lady of the Reich, encouraging her to wear makeup and high-fashion clothing in stark contrast to the plain look fostered by most women in Germany. He had a mistress, Eva Braun, whom he chose to marry shortly before committing suicide. And he was sugar reactive, his mood swings often determined by the volume of candy and other sweets that he consumed.

Martin Luther King, Jr., was a brilliant orator who believed in nonviolent protest targeted toward the most outrageous examples of racial prejudice. He protested lunch counters where blacks could handle all food preparation and service but could not sit at the stools and be regular customers. He asked only for human dignity; the violence against his simple request was so obscene that individuals who would ordinarily not get involved suddenly joined the fight for civil rights. Yet he was also both a family man and a man whose close associates, including the Rev. Ralph Abernathy, accused of womanizing during his travels. He, again, was an individual who was multidimensional and all the more interesting for that reason.

And Lise Meitner split the atom, her work ensuring the creation of atomic power and atomic weapons. Yet she was denied the Nobel Prize because of sexism on the committee (the prize went to her male assistant, Otto Hahn). The emotional turmoil that was created by the snub she received for reasons unrelated to her genius created deep and lasting pain. Yet she went on with her work, never showing the bitterness that she undoubtedly held within.

The fullness of the lives of our heroes and villains makes them truly fascinating. They come alive in all their human complexity. And you, the biographer, are privileged to learn their passions, their follies, their innermost secrets.

Why should a reader care about such things? Why not limit what is written to the horrors or heroics for which the individual became of historic importance?

The truth is that individuals are far more fascinating when they are "real." It is too simple to make saints of the heroic, to give readers the impression that such individuals were unique in history, as though anointed by God to serve one purpose and one purpose only. Likewise, it is wrong to see the dastardly as inherently so evil that when their time came to rise to power, no one, no matter how strong or virtuous, could stand against them.

Unfortunately myth is sometimes celebrated as fact. Most Americans fail to recognize the name of Parson Mason Locke Weems (1759-1825) who felt that truth should never get in the way of a good story. Essentially he wrote fiction that glorified famous men, never expecting anyone to take the work as fact. It was often racy and humorous for his day, writing meant to be enjoyed rather than trusted.

So why do I mention a man whose work would not be approved today? It is because one of his books was called *The Life and Memorable Actions of George Washington*. He wrote it at a time when Washington's private life and his military skills were not that well known. The fact that he and Sally Fairfax had a relationship before his marriage to Martha, a relationship Washington considered the only happiness he had known, according to his letters, had not been discovered. The fact that Washington was not particularly respected as a general, though he was a good political compromiser and obviously had adequate leadership skills, was not discussed. So much of what today makes for fascinating reading about the man now called the "father of our country" was not yet common knowledge that Weems was at a loss for research. In addition, he wanted the Washington book to be read by young adults and felt that Washington should be a physical, moral, and spiritual example for them, regardless of the truth. As a result, and by his own admission he made up stories, never expecting anyone to take them seriously.

What were the stories? The most famous bit of nonsense was the one about George Washington chopping down the cherry tree on his father's land, then admitting it and taking his punishment. Less obvious was Washington's deep reverence, his frequent prayers for guidance, and his reliance on his religion. Nothing in Washington's extensive papers or the papers of his contemporaries indicates that Washington, the man, had any interest in religion or God whatever. There was no minister in attendance at any time while he lay dying. And when he was buried, it was with a Masonic ceremony lacking a spiritual leader. But Weems wanted children to follow God so he thought it best to have Washington be the type of man he wanted the children to emulate, even if he created a myth.

Today a man like Weems would be in trouble for such actions. At the very least, his history writing would be ridiculed by those who are knowledgeable critics in the field. At worst, he would lose any libel suit because there would be a presumption of dishonesty in his writing.

There are times when inaccuracy in writing can serve a useful purpose, though. Autobiographies of the famous are extremely important for our understanding of history. This is not because only the subject can be completely accurate, though ideally this is the case. Rather it is the fact that an autobiography is the way in which a subject wishes to be remembered by others.

For example, when former President Richard Nixon wrote his autobiography, he worked with journalist Diane Sawyer as his ghostwriter, a field that will be discussed later in this book. Many other professional writers said that they would not have worked with Nixon because they felt he would lie. Certainly such earlier books as Nixon's *Six Crises*, written when he was vice-president, had details that failed to match the facts as others knew them. Even former President Eisenhower with whom he served in office felt that Nixon's discussion of the Middle East crisis during his administration was wrong. And Eisenhower spoke out about the inaccuracy at a time when he should have been supportive of his former running mate.

Yet there were other voices being heard. It was felt by many biographers that the Nixon autobiography was important because it provided the former president's view of how he wanted to be remembered. It would not be trusted as an accurate document of history. Rather, it would be seen as a document that reflected the aspects of his administration he felt should be emphasized and the way he wanted to receive credit. Given those circumstances, the writers all felt that they would have been pleased to act as a "ghost."

There are other reasons for writing biographies and as-told-to autobiographies. Sometimes they are as simple as the fact that someone lived, was important to a group of people, and those people wanted that individual remembered.

For example, many historical societies commission biographies of individuals who are important to their community. They want to remember the person who founded an area, who ran the largest business, who developed the land and created a community from the wilderness. These people are not important on a national scale. There would be no market for a biography sold throughout the United States. But within the community, such individuals have played roles that should be remembered and the society tries to act as the vehicle for having a book commissioned.

No matter who you may choose to write about, no matter whether the person is internationally known or merely important to a limited number of individuals, biographies and as-told-to autobiographies can be the most interesting, exciting, and challenging works you will ever produce.

Do I Need to Be a Name?

If you are a new writer, or if you have written but never tried a biography or as-told-to autobiography, one concern you will have is whether or not anyone will be interested in your work. Don't I have to have a "name"? you might ask.

The truth is that "names" do not sell books to the general public. For example, if I mention William Novak, would you have any idea who he might be? Chances are that you would say you have never heard of him. Or perhaps his name sounds familiar from "something," but you have no idea what he might have written. Yet if I mentioned Lee Iacocca; Sidney Biddle Barrows, the Mayflower Madam; or Nancy Reagan, you would immediately recognize their names and the fact that they all are the authors of best-selling books.

Iacocca, Barrows, Reagan, and others are *not* authors, though. They are the subjects of as-told-to autobiographies actually written by Bill Novak whom you will meet later in this book. Novak wrote their stories for them, but it was not the Novak name that made them best sellers. The subjects were the only ones of interest.

This is true for every writer in this field. When I first was on the *New York Times* Best Seller List for my as-told-to autobiography *DeLorean*, people were shocked to discover that I had written the book. My name was on the cover with John DeLorean's. My name was included on the best seller lists alongside John's. But what people remembered was that the innovative car designer/manufacturer arrested, then acquitted, for a drug deal some government agents set up, had written a book. My name's existence on the cover was but a trivia question.

If you select a subject in whom people are interested, it is the subject, not your name, that will sell the book. Only on rare occasions, such as Alex Haley, author of *Roots*, will the author be as important as the subject, a status reserved for literally a handful of writers who have been marketed in much the same manner as their subjects.

There is a difference between the experienced writer and the beginner when it comes to handing out contracts. Publishers know that books are major undertakings. The research can take months or longer to complete; the writing many weeks more. Someone who has written other books understands the process, is used to budgeting time, and is likely to meet the deadline without a problem. A beginner might become overwhelmed by the process, quitting the writing before the book is completed. As a result, a new writer may be asked to complete the bulk of a book before a contract is given. By contrast, an experienced writer may obtain a contract based solely on a brief proposal.

Yet both writers will ultimately receive contracts and have their books published. Both writers will make their sales based on the subjects of their books. And both writers will stand an equal chance at becoming major successes. The only difference is the stage within the writing process when this takes place. Publishers expect to see more pages of writing as the sample sent by an unknown than they need to see from someone who has one or more published biographies to his or her credit. Thus no matter what your level of professional recognition, you *can* sell your biography or as-told-to autobiography.

What About Money?

As I write this book, I have before me the latest best seller list put out by *Publishers Weekly*, the trade journal for the publishing business. There are fifteen hard-cover books on the list. Five of them are biographies or as-told-to autobiographies. This is one-third of the books most in demand in bookstores throughout the United States.

Not every book reaches the list, of course. There are more than 48,000 new book titles in the average year, a fact that shows that biographies account for a disproportionate number of successes. At the same time, there are many biographies that will sell a few thousand copies and never be seen again.

Today publishers enthusiastically embrace biographies, paying a disproportionate advance for such works. Sometimes this is quite low, five thousand or ten thousand dollars for the work, because the marketing department indicates that the book may not earn back more than this amount. At other times the fee is quite high, six figures or more for a person of great interest. Kitty Kelley received well over a million dollars for her unauthorized, but thoroughly researched and documented, biography of Frank Sinatra. And while that money had to pay for research, extensive travel, legal fees, and other expenses much higher than the average person could even conceive of incurring, the publisher provided the money with the expectation that the sales would be so great, that money and more would be earned back through sales.

You cannot write a book for the money. You have to think only of your reader, not personal gain. If you do not entertain, inform, and hopefully fascinate your reader with the story you have to tell, the book will not sell. But once you focus on your reader, once you are working in this field, you will find that the rewards are often far greater than those for any other category of book you might try.

Selecting a Subject

I n theory, anyone who interests you as a possible subject for a biography will also interest a great many others. The facts that caused you to say to yourself, "That's fascinating! I'd love to read a book about that person" should be enough to sell your book. While the reality is slightly more complicated than that, a fact that will be discussed shortly, in general, the logic of such reasoning is correct. Thus let us explore the different types of biographies you might consider.

Types of Biographies

There are several types of biographies. If you are writing about an individual who is currently alive, there are authorized and unauthorized biographies. An authorized biography has the subject's cooperation. He or she will grant you one or more interviews and will also help you interview friends, acquaintances, co-workers, and others who are familiar with that person's life and work.

An authorized biography is *not* the same as an as-told-to autobiography. An as-told-to book is the subject's story. You interview the subject exclusively, usually doing little outside research except to confirm dates or other facts. Then you tell that subject's story in his or her own words. When the subject appears on talk shows, the person who has read the book should feel that the way the person sounds on the air is identical to the way he or she came across in the book. You write in the subject's voice, not your own.

The unauthorized biography may or may not be written with the aid of interviews of your subject. You are writing about the person, talking with friends, acquaintances, co-workers, and anyone else you can find who will talk with you. Such books may be more accurate than an authorized biography because there is no interference on the part of those biased in the subject's favor. On the other hand, they may be inaccurate because the subject refuses to talk with you, and the people who could give you a balanced story are unwilling to speak.

Kitty Kelley is one of the most successful writers of unauthorized biographies, having produced works on Elizabeth Taylor, Jackie Kennedy, Frank Sinatra, and Nancy Reagan, among others. She is also considered one of the most careful researchers in the business. She makes notes every time she telephones anyone in conjunction with a book she is writing, whether or not she gets through to the person. She obtains documents, tape records all her interviews, and has not been proven to be inaccurate in terms of the facts she obtains.

Kelley's most controversial unauthorized biography was *My Way*, a massive story of Frank Sinatra that contained family details that were quite embarrassing for him. There were charges that she was wrong, that he would sue, and other allegations, none of which was ever acted upon. Yet according to people in the know, there were some unintentional inaccuracies. These were not serious and they were not the result of mistakes on Kelley's part. However, they do reveal one problem that exists for the unauthorized biographer. Not everyone involved with the subject will agree to talk with you so your information may inadvertently be one-sided.

Then there are the "literary" biographies and the biographies of individuals long dead. The former may involve going through the writings of the subject and those with whom he or she interacted. For example, Joan Richardson, an English professor in New York, produced a two-volume set of books covering the life of poet Wallace Stevens. The biography counterpoints his life with his writing. It provided a far more complete understanding of both the poetry that brought him fame and the lifestyle that kept him somewhat estranged from his wife, Elsie Stevens, an occasional artist's model whose portrait was used for both the Mercury Dime and Walking Liberty Half-Dollar created by sculptor Adolph Weinman in 1916.

There are those who write based on a different medium as well. For example, Robert Benajorun wrote a combination literary criticism and biography of Woody Allen utilizing his movies (*The Films Of Woody Allen*). In general he made an effort to both look at the life of the person, the letters and other writings of the subject, then try to show a more complete picture of the person through such analysis. Sometimes this is done with a living writer, an action that can result in problems for the writer since the subject retains the copyright on all letters. The fact that they may be owned by a library or archives does not alter the subject's right to keep the contents private, according to court cases in recent years. At other times the work is handled after the writer's death, usually with the approval of whoever controls the estate.

Other types of biographies of historic figures are researched any way possible. Newspapers are checked, as are writings of contemporaries and anything else that can be found. For example, if someone wanted to write a biography of Jesus Christ, the writer would not only study the Bible but also the writings of Flavius Josephus, a historian born in A.D. 37 whose work has survived. In addition, there are histories of Rome and the Middle East, scrolls from the period that were discovered in recent decades, and numerous other works that reveal the life and/or the times. Each period of history has its own resources, a situation that will be explored in chapter three.

Historical biographies are sometimes the easiest to write, not because the skills are less involved but because the information is both known and limited. There is no one alive to interview. Any travel that must be done is to locations where records are maintained or where you can see the land that was a part of the person's life. It is sometimes possible to do all of your research within one city, especially when the entire written record of the person's life has been collected by a library, museum, or similar archives. This can save you large sums of money over time.

Selecting Your Subject

There are numerous ways to select a subject for a biography. Some writers specialize in a field of personal interest—rock music stars, literary greats of the 1920s, presidents of the United States, or some other areas. Others, such as myself, will tackle any project that seems interesting, fun to research, and a challenge to write. In addition, there are those who are obsessed with one person, who are driven to tell a specific story and may or may not write again.

Scott Berg began his career as a "driven" author, though he has since become a well-established professional. He became fascinated with the famous Scribner's editor Max Perkins, the man who guided the careers of Ernest Hemingway, F. Scott Fitzgerald, and others. And that obsession begun while he was a college student at Princeton University, eventually became a best-selling biography. As he described it:

"While at Princeton I kept pawing my way through the [F. Scott] Fitzgerald archives and kept finding the most intriguing stuff there was the F. Scott Fitzgerald–Maxwell Perkins correspondence. Then Carlos Baker was teaching at Princeton and he had just finished his Hemingway biography. I introduced myself to him because I thought, being an English major, it would be kind of wonderful if he'd be my adviser. And I began doing a lot of Hemingway reading and all that under him. Then one day I came to him and said I have a great idea for a book.

"This would have been about the middle of my sophomore year. It occurred to me that there could be a book on Max Perkins. And he said, yes, that was a great idea, but why didn't I try it as a senior thesis first since I'd never written anything in my life. And second, he said, 'Have you read Thomas Wolfe yet?'

"I said, no, I've never read Wolfe.

"And he said, 'How can you write about Perkins if you've never read Wolfe? That's the real heart of the story.'

"I went off for two weeks and just read Thomas Wolfe. Nobody ever saw me. And I fell madly in love with Wolfe. It was just incredible. I felt that somehow, God, this is just something I've got to do. I became obsessed with Max Perkins."

Berg read Wolfe's four novels, then discovered that the Scribner family (founders of Charles Scribner's Sons, Publishers) had just given the bulk of their archives to the Princeton library. "There sitting in Firestone Library were the originals of every letter Max Perkins received—Max Perkins among many Scribner editors—and carbon copies of every letter he sent out, including a great part of the Wolfe archives."

Berg was nineteen at the time. He spent his last two years in Princeton going through the resources whenever he had time.

The senior thesis was normally not an involved project. Most of the students started during their last semester, the total length being 45 to 60 pages. Berg worked more than two years and wrote 250 pages, the basis for what would be his book. It also was the longest senior thesis in Princeton history, though Berg felt that he had only scratched the surface of Maxwell Perkins.

"I said to Carlos Baker, I figure I can have this book out in nine months," said Berg, discussing his reaction to the positive comments concerning his thesis.

"I said, I figure I can research for three months, I'll write for three months, and it will be published in three months. That's how dumb I was."

Berg graduated June 8, 1971, then went to the Princeton library the next morning to begin research on the book. He worked every day, his parents providing him food and shelter in the same manner that they would have done had he gone to graduate school. "I traveled for a year and a half doing research. I took buses and lived on the couches of friends. The Perkins family, when I went to interview them, put me up. They were extraordinarily generous." Yet despite his enthusiasm, it was not until 1975 that he signed the contract for the book. And it was not until 1978 that Dutton issued *Max Perkins, Editor of Genius* by A. Scott Berg. The book was a major best seller and has sold well ever since.

Berg's selection of a subject was obviously the result of an impassioned youth. However, the book's success was the result of more than skilled writing. Dutton's marketing department had little sense of the potential of the volume. They wanted to produce a small number of copies, then be done with it. Instead, Berg used contacts from his father, a motion picture and television producer, in order to get on radio and television talk shows. His publicity efforts were effective enough to begin boosting sales, at which time the publisher decided to financially support the publicity for the project.

By contrast to Berg's experience, Neil Baldwin, the author of biographies on Man Ray and William Carlos Williams, commented: "Nobody should start out writing a biography unless they really, truly would practically kill to write it. I think anything short of that does a disservice to yourself and to the subject and to the reader. I got into this thing, and I got about two-thirds of the way into it and it looked like it would never end. And I said well . . . But I was so into it, I didn't feel like I was being tortured. I mean, it was very hard, but I wanted, deeply wanted to write it. And I'm not going to write another book until that same feeling is back, and it might take me another couple of years."

Baldwin was not a full-time writer when *Man Ray* was released, but the book's success was such that he began receiving requests for another book. The offers were tempting, but there were sacrifices he had to consider. "I started thinking, do I really want to give up every weekend, every vacation, every morning at five o'clock in the morning. You know, no more hanging out with anybody. No more going to a movie or something.

"You really have to want to kill to write. I don't know how else to put it. Otherwise it's not going to work.

"I think in biography you have to go with this omnivorous feeling. I know that I have read everything. I know that I have talked with almost everyone who I could get my hands on. I know that I have read every word that was written by or about Man Ray. I know that is the case. And that is the only way that I could do a book on anybody. So until that comes up again, I won't be doing another book on anyone."

For Ken Turan, being a journalist helped him make contact with actress Patty Duke (*Call Me Anna: The Autobiography of Patty Duke*). "I started with an article I did for *TV Guide*. I was on the staff of *TV Guide* at that point in time. She was in a new series and they sent me to do the usual kind of interview that you do. There was just something about her story that intrigued me." He talked about the couple who were acting coaches who discovered her and manipulated her as a child, creating what she later came to consider a total lie.

"The story really intrigued me. I'd done many, too many of these stories where people have all degrees of fame and obscurity. And this was really the first time I'd come away and said, there's a book here and I'd like to do it." It turned out that Patty Duke had had similar thoughts. Ultimately she and Ken came to terms for a project that became a best seller.

Over the years I have found that most people are the same way. They have a story that they want to tell. You are a writer without a story. They cannot write and you have not lived their life. The match is perfect and the response is frequently favorable.

Oddly this is true with celebrities, not just the average person who has an unusual achievement. I am a member of Writer's Guild of America, West, the screenwriter's guild. This means that I have sold enough projects to the television and film industry so that I am both eligible for membership and required to join. However, in the eyes of film people, I am different. As one explained, "We have hundreds of people out here who can write a script. But you're special. You write books. You're a *real* writer."

The reality is nonsense, of course. Some of the finest writers in the country write screenplays. It is the image that people in film and television have that affects you and it is the reason why many entertainment figures use inexperienced authors, something you would not expect to occur.

Unauthorized biographies of living subjects often do not result in the subject's cooperation. However, you will find that when you begin talking with friends and acquaintances of the subject, most will talk freely. Sometimes they are hostile, other times they are friendly. But usually they will talk.

The most important point is that you must make an effort to research the book through interviews where possible, and through libraries, archives, and similar locations otherwise. Do not worry whether or not someone will cooperate. Do not worry about your experience. Select your subject and begin the work. If you are interested, if you can justify the interest of others for the marketing department, you will get published.

But what if you just want to write a biography and have no specific subject in mind? All you know for certain is that you want the person to be living and unusual enough to sustain your interest during the long and sometimes tedious research process. The following questions to ask yourself should help you as you read newspapers, magazines, and other sources while looking for a contemporary subject about whom to write.

1. Has the person had experiences with enough depth to warrant a book? Age is not a factor. For example, a sports biography often covers someone who may be only twenty-five or thirty years old. However, such an individual has had to rise through amateur competition to the ranks of either Olympic or professional athletics. Such experiences have taken the athlete into worlds the average person can only imagine.

2. Is the story a dramatic one that will sustain interest throughout the book? As I write this, the Associated Press wire service has sent an article throughout the country about Michael Shannon, a nineteen-year-old American dancer from Los Angeles. In theory he is too young to warrant a book. But consider his story.

   Michael was fourteen when he left home to become a world-class dancer. His mother understood his dream, knew she could not persuade him to wait, and accepted his decision. His talent enabled him to gain jobs and training as a dancer in the United States, Canada, Sweden, Hungary, Finland, Italy, Austria, Czechoslovakia, Bulgaria, and the Soviet Union. His art defied politics and he survived by learning to speak Russian, Hungarian, and Italian in addition to his native English.

   Michael returned to the United States at nineteen, touring with the Bolshoi Ballet Academy, perhaps the most prestigious ballet company in the world. It appears that he will be asked to join the main company of the Bolshoi Ballet, an honor that is unique for an American. That triumph, coupled with the drama of traveling the world for five years in order to reach the top of his art, is an obvious book. Nineteen-year-old Michael Shannon has had more interesting experiences in the most recent five years of his life than many individuals in their sixties.

   In addition, the market for books about ballet is known, the audience is large enough to warrant publishing interest. Because of the dancer's age, the book will also fit the young adult (teenager) market. Thus it is a good biography to consider writing.

3. Can you define the audience in terms of other books on similar subjects, organizations that might be interested in promoting it, business and/or hobby trends, or other reasons? If the audience requires nontraditional marketing, such as direct mail, can you pinpoint exactly how to sell it? The ballet star mentioned in point 2 is a good example. A religious leader obviously is of interest to the members of the religion where he or she became famous. A colorful character from the Old West will be of interest to the reader of true West magazines, history buffs, and others. Advertisements in magazines related to the West and American history, direct mail to subscribers, and other nontraditional approaches to sales could be used if the publisher can work that way (see chapter eleven, "Selling the Biography"). The more you are able to define your market, the easier it will be to make a sale.
4. Are there other books currently in the marketplace that should be considered direct competition? As you will see in chapter eleven, you are not competing with all the biographies ever written. You are competing only with those books available in the bookstores today. If there is too much competition, your book will not sell. However, books are cyclical. Periods of great interest are followed by periods when there is little or nothing on a given topic. Such cycles generally follow one-and-a-half-year periods. If there is too much competition today, within no more than a year-and-a-half you will find that the market is wide open again.

In addition, you may find that your angle is uniquely different. I wanted to write about New York in the 1940s, only to find that there were several books that included this period. However, no one had written about it through the eyes of Arthur Fellig, a rather disreputable photographer who recorded the extremes of New York society using the name "Weegee, the famous." By using a biography of Weegee as the vehicle for showing New York during World War II, I made the sale.

By contrast, an artist's biography did not sell until I agreed to write about the era with my subject as a major vehicle. In both cases, a slight change in emphasis sold the book.

5. If your subject is truly unknown, can you generate interest through other forms of writing? Sometimes the placement of articles concerning your subject can turn an obscure individual into a national figure in whom there is greater publishing

interest (see chapter ten, "Creating a Market for Your Book").

6. Why are you interested in your subject? What makes knowing the life of this person so compelling that you are willing to take the time and effort needed to tell the story in an interesting, effective manner? When you have difficulty answering the previous questions, sometimes taking a fresh look at your subject through your own eyes at the time you decided to write the book will give you the answers you seek. Remember that you are typical of your readers. Think about your own interest and the other issues often resolve themselves.

Finally, once you make your decision, do not be concerned about anything except moving forward with the work. If you are fascinated enough with someone else's life to do the research that will result in his or her biography, you can be certain that eventually others will share your interest and it will sell.

Defining Your Subject

1. In what field is the person known, if any? Sports? Medicine? Theater? Movies? Television? Education? Politics? The military? Space exploration? Business? Organized crime? Art? Dance? Literature? Etc.
2. What incident, heroic action, personal experience, or related circumstance has made your subject of national interest? (This may or may not relate to question 1.)
3. If the subject is an unknown with a fascinating story, has there been local, regional, and/or national publicity generated about the person? If so, what kind? Where? How recent? If not, is the situation current enough so that such publicity could be generated?
4. Are there special interest groups that might want to publicize the biography? These might range from organizations fighting a particular disease to ethnic/American groups that relate to the subject.
5. Are there other countries where interest might be high for the subject? If so, list them. Also list anything you know about special interest areas within that country, such as the American West club that exists in Germany.
6. If the subject is a familiar one, what new slant will you be bringing to the book? Newly discovered papers and/or archives? Interviews with people who have not discussed the subject in the past? A new interpretation, perhaps by bringing

together a combination of resources in a different manner?

7. Is there anything that makes you unusually qualified to write this biography? Special educational background? A relationship with the subject? Access to interviews others have not obtained? An unusual amount of research involving resources others have yet to tap? (These circumstances are not critical. They are extras, but you do not need them in order to make the sale.) A special relationship with the subject or a relationship with someone who maintained such a relationship?

8. Can you justify the fact that the book will be of interest in two or more years? This may have to do with the historical importance of the person or the unusual quality of the story. It may have to do with an anniversary that is coming up. Or there may be some other factor. What matters is that the interest will not be over by the time the book can be completed, printed, warehoused, distributed, promoted, and sold.

Historic Figures

Historic figures seem harder to write about than contemporary subjects, if only because there are so many books already available on many of them. Frequently experts in the field are discouraging because they talk about how there is no way to write a better book on Lincoln (or Nero or Saint Francis, or whomever) than the one written by Professor Knowitall of Harvard University in 1933. They forget that in the business of publishing, competition means the books currently in print. Perhaps Professor Knowitall's book is the definitive one, but if you cannot buy it in a bookstore, if you must seek it in libraries, then it might as well not exist.

Children's books offer more competition with familiar names than do adult books. This is because such books are kept in print longer. Yet children's book editors stress that their books are so relatively short that they can cover only one aspect of the person's life. This is why there might be a biography of Lincoln that is rather general, another one that deals with Lincoln only as president, and yet another about what it was like to be a boy when Lincoln was growing up, all by the same publisher.

Adult books, too, provide many opportunities. Suppose you are fascinated by presidential campaigns but feel that the presidents who interest you are too well known to write a book about them. You might write a collective biography called "The Also Rans," telling the stories of some of the more colorful, yet long-forgotten losers.

Using Lincoln again, there might be a book along the lines of

"The Unknown Lincoln: The Time Before the War." Or you might explore the lives of Lincoln's children to see what happened to them after their father was shot.

Each person's life has the potential for more than one approach. In addition, you may find that there is previously unused material available. Sometimes this comes from newly released documents that were sealed during the lifetime of various heirs. At other times the material comes from people who were contemporaries of the subject yet whose papers were not explored. You may find a treasure trove of correspondence that was previously hidden.

Perhaps equally important is one last fact. A writer who produces an interesting, readable book, well researched and in a style that makes it fun for the casual reader as well as the "buff," will find a ready market. It does not matter what competition is out there, except for the fact that you may have to delay your sale a few months until the competing title is off the market. But the delay is a minor problem. What matters is that if a subject interests you enough to write about the person, and if your writing is of good quality, you will sell the book. I have done it along with thousands of others over the years. And this book will help you succeed as well.

A Walk on the Technical Side

Now that you have selected the subject about which you wish to write, it is important to understand what you will be facing with your submission. You need to have a sense of how publishing companies, in general, operate. While there are many differences among them, and not all have the same staff positions, the following is an overview of what you will face and how you can make your presentation so that you will ultimately triumph in your goal to sell your book.

Publishing Company Divisions

There are three divisions within a book publishing company that affect you, the writer. The first is editorial. This is where the book is first read by an editor, editorial assistant, or reader. The latter, when such a person exists, is someone who is usually new to the company, understands what types of books are desired, and handles the preliminary screening of the books that come into the offfices unsolicited. The reader's job is to reject the badly written and inappropriate books, then pass along the remainder to the editor. The assistant editor's job, when the position exists, is somewhat similar, though an assistant editor is usually more knowledgeable and may reject a few more manuscripts than the reader might.

Equally important, if the assistant editor feels strongly that a book should be published, the editor will listen seriously.

Ultimately the decision to publish is made by the editor, sometimes in conjunction with an editorial board. This is the person who is astute, perceptive, intelligent, cultured, and a truly great human being when your book is accepted. The editor becomes an unthinking dolt with no taste and no future should your book be rejected. Either way, the contract will be negotiated by the editor who will then act as midwife as you give birth to your manuscript.

The publicist is the person who will be promoting the book. This is the individual who coordinates all advertising, any author tour, telephone interviews, and whatever else may be utilized to get the book attention from the media and the public.

The marketing department may or may not be separate from publicity. It is the marketing department's job to get the book into the stores before the publicity brings it to the public's attention. Marketing makes certain that the retailers are familiar with the book and, ideally, convinces them to take several volumes for their shelves. No matter what else takes place, if the marketing department is not enthusiastic, the book will not get into the stores. If the book is not in the stores, it will not sell.

But don't all bookstores stock all books? No, and reasons are many, the most important being the lack of space.

Suppose a bookstore is of a size where it can sell approximately ten thousand different titles at any given time. If you divide the more than forty-eight thousand new titles into the twelve months of a calendar year, this means that more than four thousand titles appear approximately every thirty days. If the stores turned over their new titles every month, it might be possible for a store with room for ten thousand different titles to always have the latest books. However, people do not go into bookstores just to buy the latest books. They want other products and these also take extensive space.

For example, suppose you delight in Agatha Christie mysteries. The paperback section of your bookstore may have a dozen of her titles at any given time. Yet Agatha Christie has been dead for several years and the titles are all those of books completed in the past. Edgar Rice Burroughs has been dead for many years, yet his Tarzan and science fiction works are constantly in demand.

Other writers are the same, whether living authors who have been publishing for some time or long-dead writers whose work has endured. Older work is on the shelves, taking space. In addition, there are dictionaries and reference works, as well as nonbook items such as videos and blank "books" that are meant to be used as diaries. All together, some smaller bookstores report that as few as one-third of their current holdings represent new books.

This situation is not a bad one. For example, newer readers may become intrigued by a series such as *Sweet Valley High* or *Nancy Drew*, delighting in one book, then wanting to read everything that came before. Once "hooked" on books, they will branch out into other areas, becoming the major buyers of tomorrow. In addition, such practices assure current writers that there may be a market for their own previous works. Such previous works kept in print form what publishers call their backlist and the sales from the backlist assure you a steady income as you produce new projects. Unfortunately every older backlist book on the shelf means less room for a new one. The marketing department recognizes this fact and tries to find ways to be certain a new book will get shelf space.

The "Dreaded Marketing Department"

The first concern a marketing department has is whether or not the staff feels there is a market for a certain type of book. Currently, and for the foreseeable future, biography and as-told-to autobiography are fields for which there is predicted great success. These are categories expected to be as enduring as romance, mysteries, and even diet books. But there was a time when this was not the case.

Several years ago I encountered a story about a man who was a multiple personality. He had at least five different "people" living quite separate lives within his body. The man, Henry Hawksworth, was the first male so diagnosed who received any sort of national attention and I worked with him to write his autobiography, *The Five of Me*.

I wrote the proposal, a lengthy one that was also the best I had ever written at that time. I sent it to Arco Publishing Company, which had been publishing this type of book. (Note: Companies change their emphasis from time to time. Arco has not been associated with biographies for several years now but, at the time, this was appropriate for their list.) The editor wrote back with great enthusiasm. He loved the book. He wanted to publish the book. He thought it was fabulous. But . . .

The "but" came from the "Dreaded Marketing Department," which said that the market for books had changed in the United States. Two years earlier they could have sold an autobiography of this type, but the market had shifted. Bookstores wouldn't stock *The Five of Me*. The public would not be interested. They could not sell the book.

Frustrated, certain that the "Dreaded Marketing Department"

never makes a mistake, I nonetheless contacted Contemporary Books to see what they would think. Their editor was equally enthusiastic, though he also turned it over to the "Dreaded Marketing Department." I thought I was doomed. I knew that marketing is an extremely scientific business and that if one department says there is no market for a certain type of book, there is no market for such a book.

To my amazement, Contemporary Books' marketing experts did not know *The Five of Me* could not sell. Even more amazing, Pocket Books made the same "mistake," bringing out the book in paperback a year after the hardback was in the stores. And even more amazing, CBS Television was "foolish" enough to buy the rights to the book and turn it into a Movie-of-the-Week that received a rave review from *People* magazine.

So what is the point of all this? First, you have to constantly be aware that you must justify the potential for selling a book to the marketing department. This is the most important lesson and a critical one to remember.

However, you must also remember that if you feel you can justify the sales of a book, you should not give up as a result of just one rejection. The conclusions of one company's staff are not necessarily going to be the conclusions reached by the staff of a different company.

Justifying Sales

The first concern the marketing department has is who will care about your subject. Is the person about whom you wish to write a national figure? If not, did the individual do something that brought the subject to national attention?

Should you be writing for a more specialized market, such as the religious field, the question becomes whether or not the subject will be known to that more narrow audience. The life of a saint may have limited national appeal. But if the saint is important to the Catholic Church, and if you are trying to sell your book to a publisher specializing in books for Catholics, you probably will have met one of your marketing tests.

Is the subject of regional interest? Sometimes the story of someone famous within a particular city or region of the country will sell provided the publisher can market to that area. Contemporary Books published a successful book about the first woman mayor of Chicago, though the book sold almost exclusively within a few Illinois cities. The print run was kept to a level where it matched local interest in an area that had a large enough population base to make it profitable. It was not a national biography, but it was a highly salable one.

Is the subject unknown but the period of history of such interest that a book is worth publishing? As I write this, I am under contract to tell the story of Count Folke Bernadotte of Sweden. You have probably never heard of him, yet he was a major figure in the rescue of thirty thousand people from the concentration camps at the end of World War II. He was almost single-handedly responsible for helping to turn Heinrich Himmler against Hitler in the last days of the Reich, perhaps saving thousands more lives.

Bernadotte is not a famous name, but his work and the people with whom he interacted are so famous (or infamous) that the marketing department felt the book would sell well. In addition, there is a strong European market for the book where Bernadotte *is* known. The publisher, Paragon House, expects to sell the book internationally, placing articles related to the story in American publications to boost awareness.

Later in this book you will learn how to build the appeal for what you write. For now, though, it is enough to be aware that you will have to justify why the book will sell. This is quite simple when writing about a famous name. It is more difficult when you are dealing with a relative unknown who has led a fascinating life. However, if you can convince the Dreaded Marketing Department that there is a predictably sizable group of readers for what you wish to sell, there will be a publishing company willing to take a chance on you.

THREE

Gaining the Cooperation of the As-Told-To Subject

Y ou talk to celebrities all the time," said a student at a writer's seminar where I was speaking. "But I wouldn't know how to locate someone famous. How do you do it? Do you develop some sort of list over the years or what?"

The secret, I explained, was a book I discovered several years ago. Anyone who opens the book will find the home or business numbers of the majority of the wealthy, the famous, and the infamous. It is a book I have used successfully with movie stars, broadcasting executives, politicians, doctors, lawyers, and others in the news. While there are times it has failed me, those times are few and far between. More important, there have always been alternative ways to reach the people.

"So how do you get this book?" the student asked, a little annoyed with me. She thought that either I was not telling the truth or it was a volume whose distribution was carefully controlled to ensure the privacy of the people listed within. "I don't suppose a beginning writer is even allowed to know the title of it."

The book is free, I explained. And many larger libraries carry the regional editions for the different parts of the country. As to the title, that is no secret, either. It is called the telephone directory.

I would like to say that the student stared at me in amazement, her jaw slack, her eyes registering shock. I would like to say that her surprise turned to understanding, a smile crossing her lips as she said, "My God, that's so easy. Why didn't I think of it?" I'd like to say that, but it didn't happen that way. Instead the student looked coldly at me and stated:

"You know, you professionals are all a bunch of smartasses. I paid a lot of money to hear you speak and all you want to do is keep your secrets to yourselves. You don't want to tell us the truth, that's fine. Just say you don't want to reveal your secrets. We'd understand. But don't give me that bullshit!"

It was my turn to act amazed. I had just told the students the truth and they failed to believe me.

Fact: Nobody starts off famous.

Fact: Almost everyone likes to be in the telephone book so that their friends and family can reach them.

Fact: Old habits die hard. As someone becomes famous and/or important, they still see themselves as being who and what they were before they found success. They may delight in the trappings, but a gnawing little voice inside their head keeps reminding them that at any moment they might be unmasked as a fraud. They might discover that they are little more than a big version of the frightened little boy or girl they were when growing up in Dead-at-Night, Idaho. Thus they do not follow the presumed trappings of success such as having an unlisted number.

For example, Helen Hayes is one of the most prominent actresses on Broadway and has been for more than thirty years. Her name has long meant box office success. Her face has appeared on seemingly countless magazine covers. She also has been listed in the Manhattan telephone directory all that time. She even joked about the situation with Johnny Carson on "The Tonight Show."

Helen Hayes is not unusual. People of prominence have to be accessible. If they aren't, they become trivia questions to be mentioned at parties and in bars.

Whenever I want to reach someone, whether rich and famous or an average person who was suddenly thrown into fame and fortune by an unusual life circumstance, the first thing I do is check the telephone book for wherever they live. In the case of Hollywood stars, I will check several directories including the various Los Angeles directories, the ones for Hollywood, Beverly Hills, and similar surrounding locations. Larger city libraries and many university libraries maintain either the books or microfiche versions of the books. Should I be in an area where this is not possible, I call the information operator for each of the cities. In at least 95 percent of the cases, that is as far as you need to go.

But what if you are not so lucky? What if you find that the person is not listed?

Call the operator anyway. Some people refuse to allow their number to be given out. Others arrange for the operator to provide it to anyone who calls, though it will not be listed in the directory (some telephone companies make a distinction between unlisted and unpublished).

The next step is to consider who the person is. Actors, actresses, and others involved with radio, television, motion pictures, and theater have to belong to one of several unions. These include Screen Actors Guild (film), Actors Equity (stage), American Federation of Radio and Television Artists (also listed as AFTRA — radio and television), the Producers Guild, the Directors Guild, and so forth. Each trade in Hollywood, from cinematographers to lighting personnel to the editors, belongs to a union, as do most people employed in the television business. The unions maintain files of members' addresses and telephone numbers that must be made available. Sometimes these are personal. At other times the people list their agents, managers, or lawyers, though mail contact is passed on to the individual involved.

Writers have guilds, too. I am a member of Writers Guild of America, West (screenwriters), Authors Guild (books), and Mystery Writers of America (mystery and suspense fiction/nonfiction). There are also several other organizations such as PEN, ASCAP, etc. Many of these are listed in the annually updated *Writer's Market*. Others can be found in lists of associations your reference librarian can provide you.

Getting a little more practical about the entertainment industry, let's explore the many ways to run down someone in the business.

First, how do you know about this person? Is it through a movie? A play? A television program? A record? A concert? A book? An interview you read in the newspaper or a magazine? A talk show on which the person was a guest?

Contact the location where you learned about the individual. If it was from a movie, find out who produced the movie (the theater manager where it was shown can give you that information) and contact the production company. (Call Los Angeles information. If that does not work, have the reference librarian at your nearest larger library show you how to locate such companies.) The company will put you in touch with the person or his/her manager, agent, and/or publicist.

The same is true for other areas. Contact the manager of the theater where the play was staged. Contact the publicity department of the publishing company that published the book. Contact the editorial department of the magazine to locate the writer of the article. Contact the managing editor of the newspaper unless it is obvious that the interviewer was a staff person. Contact the publicity department of the record company. All of these will either work or you will be referred appropriately.

Should you have any problems, go to the secretary for the president of the company (managing editor of a newspaper or magazine). I apologize for contacting the secretary, explain the problem I am having, and ask for a referral. Invariably I get it because the secretary to the person at the top is almost always unusually friendly and helpful. This is because he or she has to be unusually skilled in order to have so important a position. In fact, in some companies, the executive secretary has a better chance of becoming the boss than some of the immediate underlings. In addition, this person is accustomed to handling pressure and is concerned with the corporate image. It is a situation that you can exploit for your own benefit.

How willing to give out information are the companies? Far more willing than you would imagine, though whether this is because few people ask them or because the celebrities encourage it, I do not know.

For example, while writing the story of the Hillside Strangler, a California serial killer, I had the idea that I should learn more about the victims. I thought that if I could recreate their lives effectively, the reader might have a better sense of the tragedy of the violence. I wanted the reader to care for the victims and share in the anguish of their loss. Eventually I chose not to use this approach for a number of reasons that are not appropriate here, but the reason I mention this is because one of the victims was Jane King.

Jane King had an interesting background. She was twenty-seven, though she looked ten years younger the night she was kidnapped and murdered. She was a would-be actress with limited credits. She was a member of the Church of Scientology, a highly controversial organization. And she had lived with Mick Jagger, the leader of the rock group the Rolling Stones, eventually becoming the subject of the song "Lady Jane."

Contacting people in Hollywood who might have known Jane King proved futile. Few people admitted to knowing her and, among those who did, she came across as being rather nondescript. Instead of finding depth from which I could manipulate my readers' emotions, I had a two-dimensional character. Even listening to the song "Lady Jane" meant little because it was a meaningless song. It was one of those short, worthless numbers that groups often write when they find that they are two or three minutes shy of completing an album. Such songs are not released as singles and few people ever remember either the music or the lyrics.

I finally decided to call Mick Jagger. He knew Jane and perhaps would have some insight. If I could even figure out where he lived.

My first step was to call the program director for a rock music–oriented radio station in Tucson, Arizona, where I was living at the time. The station was the one that advertised it sponsored the Rolling Stones concerts when they were held in that city so I knew they had had contact with the Stones. To my surprise, the program director was of no help whatever.

"Oh, we don't call the Rolling Stones," he said in what I felt was a rather condescending manner. "They're famous. They call us.

We don't call them. You can't call them. No one can call them. They're famous."

It turned out that the manager for the Rolling Stones arranged their tour appearances. The shows were always so successful in Tucson that no one worried about them. A time was set, the location confirmed, hotel rooms arranged, and the station handled local promotion. But the station personnel never bothered to get contact numbers.

Certain that there had to be a better way, I went to the local record store and found the group's latest album. I noted the record company, then called the reference librarian at the public library. She gave me the address and telephone number of the company and I called the company's publicity department.

I just said that I was a writer trying to reach Mick Jagger. I said that I didn't want to interview him. I was just trying to get some information on Jane King, a murder victim with whom he had lived at one time, writing a song about her. I did not mention the book, my contract, or anything else. In fact, I was so neurotic that I felt certain I was going to be told I couldn't have any contact with Jagger or anyone associated with him.

The publicist did not ask for credentials. The publicist did not ask for whom I was writing about Jane King. She just gave me a Manhattan, New York, telephone number to call.

"What is it?" I asked. "His manager? His agent?"

"It's his New York apartment," she told me. "He'll either answer it himself or the housekeeper will get it if he's on the road. She can give you a number where you can reach him if he'll be traveling for a while so you can do your interview."

And that was all there was to it. I wanted an interview. I asked. I received.

Now before you decide that you can't have the same success, it is important to examine the reasons why "names" will talk with you. Remember I did not say that they will work with you. The decision of whether or not to grant your request to write an as-told-to autobiography or authorized biography will involve many factors. The person may even have such a project in the works. However, getting the chance to ask the person or getting the chance to do an interview related to a different subject about whom you're writing a book is fairly easy.

The reason for this is simple. How does a person become a "name"? By staying in the public eye.

My favorite female vocalist is well known for "never" giving interviews. Mention her name to journalists and everyone "knows" that she is the toughest person to reach. Her life is no longer spent on tour. She is involved with acting, producing, and other aspects of the entertainment industry. Yet when I question how the interviewer knows she does not give interviews, he or she mentions that they read a statement to that effect — in an interview. In fact, I am always delighted to read openings such as, "Although Famous Singer never gives interviews, she was gracious enough ..." Or "we got lucky and caught her on her way to ..." Or "giving her first interview in recent memory, according to Famous Singer, this reporter was told ..."

You get the idea. She makes a career of telling all comers how hard it is to get an interview with her. And she says that during the seemingly endless series of interviews she routinely provides the press.

Why does she act this way? Perhaps Famous Singer has an ego problem. Perhaps Famous Singer can't make up her mind. Or, more likely, Famous Singer has the same awareness as everyone else in the industry. If you're not constantly in the public eye, you become a trivia question to which few people will know the answer. Whatever the case, the important point is that people are easy to reach if you don't make assumptions about how hard they are to contact.

But what about people outside the entertainment world? What about the average person who accomplished something so unusual that you feel there is a book there?

Again it is a matter of going to the source. If you read the article in the newspaper, call the writer if it is a local story. If it is not, there will be either a wire service dateline (AP for Associated Press or UPI for United Press International) or a syndicate credit. Syndicates are companies such as Universal Press Syndicate, King Features Syndicate, and numerous others that supply features as fillers. Newspapers either buy a package of features or they buy them individually. Should the article have been written by a writer selling through a syndicate, the syndicate's name will be either near the byline or at the end of the article. Note what it is, then check *Writer's Market* for the address. If it is not listed, your library will have the *Editor & Publisher Syndicate Directory* that lists all syndicates and you will be able to run it down through them.

Doctors are members of the American Medical Association or the American Osteopathic Association. There will also be county or city medical societies in your area. There are associations for psychologists, psychiatrists, optometrists, chiropractors, lawyers, accountants, and other professionals should they not be listed in the telephone directory. You may have to make a few telephone calls, but knowing where you learned about an individual will enable you to contact the person.

The point is that for someone to come to your attention, someone else has written about them or they have been on or in a show you have seen. The fact that you know they exist means that you can locate them.

FOUR

Beginning the Research

T he first step in writing a biography is to recognize where you can find information resources. Even an as-told-to autobiography will require some checking. For example, Bill Novak found that when he worked with former First Lady Nancy Reagan on her memoirs, she had a poor memory for dates and details. He had to cross-check the time sequences to make certain that events they discussed were not out of order.

When I worked with John DeLorean, he had won his trial related to drug charges but was still facing other court cases. Although he would eventually triumph in all of them, those triumphs were five years away and I had six months to complete the book. I had to cross-check all his statements because the public might presume him to be lying for personal gain so all information had to be accurate.

In one instance, for example, he claimed that his ex-wife had been attending the trial in order to show off a designer's line of dresses. He said that she would arise early, carefully wash her hair and fix her makeup the way she did for a modeling assignment, then go to court in whatever dress she was supposed to be showing off that day.

Because her adultery had been one of the reasons for the breakup, I figured that he was being bitter. Even though everything else he said eventually checked out through copies of wiretap tapes, on-the-record and private testimony, court transcripts, depositions, and other resources, I was concerned that his statements about his wife were exaggerations. I assumed, like others who had watched portions of the trial, that she was simply being loyal, supportive, and friendly when photographed or being interviewed by the press. However, I called the designer in New York to check.

"Hello," I said, not giving my name. "I'm sorry to bother you, but I live in Flagstaff, Arizona [my home at the time], and my wife watched the John DeLorean trial on television. She fell in love with the clothing his wife was wearing and, when I was traveling to Beverly Hills, I heard that the clothing was supposed to be your designs. We've never seen anything like that where we live, but I travel the United States fairly regularly and can shop anywhere. If those were your clothes, I wonder where I can buy them for my wife."

"Yes," the designer said happily. "Christina Ferrare was modeling my clothing. She wore my entire fall line and you can buy it for your wife at Saks Fifth Avenue, Bloomingdales ..." And on he went, telling me the different stores in Arizona, Beverly Hills, New York, and elsewhere. The information I had been given was accurate and I could use it. Yet it did require checking.

The one problem with this was a moral one. I misrepresented myself deliberately. The facts were critical to understanding both DeLorean and a potentially libelous statement. If I was truthful about the book and the designer refused to speak with me, I would be left with an important story that I could not prove. I decided that I had less to lose through misrepresentation than through truthfulness, not a comfortable situation to be in. I can't say I made the right choice. I don't know what I will do if ever faced with the same problem. I can only be honest about what I did under the circumstances.

Other as-told-to books can be handled without such efforts. Ken Turan commented about working with Patty Duke: "I felt that this was her story. This was not pretending to be omniscient, to be a third-person biography. This was her version of events. I knew that there would be lawyers, and if the lawyers questioned anything, I was happy to have them question her about where she got it. But I didn't feel that that was my responsibility with a book of this kind. It's not like writing a journalistic story. I didn't feel the responsibility to get all sides of the story. I just got her side of the story."

But biographies, whether authorized, historical, or literary, will require careful checking. You will be working from papers, letters, books, and other documents.

Most biographies are more than the stories of individuals. They are the stories of periods of history, of communities, of events that changed lives. You cannot write about Shakespeare without having a sense of the Elizabethan era and the role of the theater in the community. A religious biographer cannot write the story of the apostle Paul without knowing the time and such communities as Corinth, Ephesus, and others where he worked and to which he wrote. And even someone such as developer for the rich, Donald Trump, cannot be understood except in the context of the sections of Manhattan where he builds and the rich who purchase his apartments.

Defining Your Research

The first step in planning your biography is to make a list of the people you will have to interview and/or the research you will have to do. First there will be the primary sources. This means your subject, if the person is alive and cooperative, but also those who were close to your subject, where appropriate.

For example, Rory Flynn decided to write a book about her late father, actor Errol Flynn. She had known him when he was alive, of course. She had his papers and other documents that her mother, one of several Flynn wives, had retained. But to make the book come alive, she knew she would have to talk with friends and acquaintances who were still alive. She defined her research by making a list of everyone she knew directly connected with the actor, where they were located if living, and where their personal papers and diaries might be found if they had died. The list ranged from producers, directors, and fellow actors, to stunt men, camera operators, technicians, and others who were involved with his pictures. Some were still relatively young. Others were in retirement, either at home or in one of the extended care facilities operated by the various motion picture unions.

It was not possible to put down all the names because many were unknown. Yet by noting the types of individuals to be contacted — technicians, supporting actors, etc. — she could then write to the various unions and seek their cooperation. Sometimes this meant having letters requesting assistance published in the bulletins produced by the guilds. At other times it meant going to the retirement areas and posting notices seeking assistance.

In addition it was necessary to locate books and archives related to individuals important to Flynn's career. These involved such subjects as Jack Warner under whom Flynn often worked. There were also archives from the various studios and books about Hollywood during the era when Flynn was active.

Additional information would come from other sources. Freedom of Information Act requests would be filed with the FBI and others in order to learn more about his less well-known past. Flynn was an adventurer in real life, his sympathies for the underdog.

This led him to Cuba during Castro's rebellion against Batista, a trip that saw him fighting with the guerrillas in the jungles in order to win what the Cubans thought would be their freedom from oppression.

Letters would also have to be dispatched to various Cuban leaders in order to try to gain their cooperation. Not everything would ultimately pay off. In fact, not every agency would cooperate within the time frame necessary to complete the book. But Rory's advance planning showed her exactly what had to be done in order to succeed.

The Freedom of Information Act

The Freedom of Information Act (FOIA) was designed to make public records available to individuals. Originally it was predominantly used by people active in the Civil Rights era to learn if the government was keeping an ongoing file of their activities. However, it served other purposes. Through FOIA, records became available that revealed wrongdoing and corruption in business and government. It was possible to review formerly classified files from the 1940s and 1950s to develop an understanding of people and events.

This is not to say that everything revealed under the Freedom of Information Act is accurate. Sometimes the case files have rumor and gossip that is not founded in fact. But even that information is of help.

For example, before starting the biography of the late actor Peter Lawford, I had his widow, Patricia S. Lawford, request Peter's FBI and Secret Service files. Among the FBI papers sent to her was a report on his friend, Marilyn Monroe. The report was one of unfounded gossip that then director J. Edgar Hoover delighted in spreading to embarrass his enemies, the Kennedy brothers. Though the data was not completely accurate, the FOIA material provided a greater understanding of the people and the times.

While the FOIA files may not be 100 percent accurate, they do reflect the information, real or alleged, that was being made available at the time. Thus these can be extremely valuable for a researcher.

There are two ways to gain information under FOIA. The first is to follow the presentation suggested by the government in a booklet available from most libraries. You can also purchase a publication on FOIA through the U.S. Government Printing Office. There are outlet locations for such documents in many federal government buildings in numerous communities. You can also write to the Printing Office in Washington, D.C. Your local library will be able to supply an address and/or telephone number.

A simpler approach is the one I have followed for several years, both for my own requests and when guiding others to make such requests. I simply write a letter to the specific agency asking for all information on a particular person, giving them as much detail as I can.

For example, suppose I want to learn whether or not there is a file for the late actor William Powell because I have heard rumors he was involved with some unsavory government activities just before World War II. I will write to all appropriate agencies I can think of, such as the FBI. An inquiry concerning someone born more recently might include additional letters to the National Security Agency and the Central Intelligence Agency. Whatever the case, I send my letter to either "Freedom of Information Act Requests," followed by the name of the agency and its address. Or I will call the agency first, find out who handles such matters, and send that person my letter directly.

Within the body of my letter I simply state:

"I am writing under the Freedom of Information Act. I would like to receive all files pertaining to the late actor William Powell." Then I will add any information I can that will pinpoint him more directly. This should include any or all of the following: 1) social security number, 2) driver's license number and state, 3) last known address or addresses, and 4) date of birth. At least one of these is usually known and that, coupled with the mention of the profession or trade, will help with the search. Providing too little information is the primary cause of being rejected.

Finally include your name and the address to which you wish to have the material sent. Type your letter neatly so it appears professional and send it off, retaining a carbon or photocopy.

There is no instant reply with a FOIA request. Response time can be many months or even a couple of years if the people handling the matter are very busy. You should receive acknowledgment of your request fairly quickly, though, usually within four to six weeks. This will just be a form stating that the agency is in receipt of your letter and will be checking their files as soon as possible.

There is a chance that an agency will say that there are no files available. Check your copy of the letter and be certain that your request contained all the information I mentioned, or as much as possible. Was the name spelled correctly? Was the date of birth accurate? What about anything else you had? If you included a social security number, were any of the digits transposed? Should there be anything wrong with your original request, send a fresh one with the correct information. If everything was fine, there is nothing more you can do even if you suspect that the agency is holding out on you.

For example, while the FBI provided Patricia Lawford with extensive material on her late husband, the U.S. Secret Service claimed that it had no files. It is possible that the Secret Service destroyed his files after his death. It is possible that the Secret Service was holding out on her. Such cynicism exists because Peter was the brother-in-law of the late President Kennedy and the Secret Service has, as one of its duties, the guarding of the president. Thus it seems unlikely that Peter was left without a Secret Service file. However there was no way to check this and she did obtain what she needed from the FBI.

There are other times when the government agency responds that the files cannot be released because of matters of national security or for some other reason. At that time you have two possible avenues of appeal. One is to appeal by letter, stating why the material should be released. The other is to go to court, the only time you will need an attorney to obtain FOIA files.

I have never had to go to the court appeal stage. Instead, I look at my request to see if there is anything wrong with it. I also consider why the request was being turned down.

How long ago was the person active in matters that might involve national security or whatever other reason has been given? There is a difference between seeking files on someone who is actively in politics or only recently retired, deceased, or otherwise out of the mainstream, and seeking them concerning someone who was active thirty years ago. You can also request all files related to matters that are not so sensitive.

For example, suppose I wanted to see the file on Clarence Kelley, the former director of the FBI. It is possible that all files related to his time as director will not be released. They could have impact on current cases, secret information that is still of importance to the government, or other matters that should not be made public record. The existence of such material could cause the FBI to make a blanket statement that the files cannot be released in the interest of national security.

It is not possible to argue with such a turndown given the nature of Kelley's work. However, it would be possible to appeal with a written request for all information that is not of a confidential nature. I might word my appeal letter as follows:

"Thank you for your response to my FOIA request [include the code number you will have been assigned at the time that your request was acknowledged originally]. I understand that there may be sensitive and confidential matters handled by Mr. Kelley during his term as FBI director. However, there will be other files that are not sensitive and material on his early life that is not confidential. Thus I am asking you to send the remainder of the material to me as required by the FOIA." In almost every case this will get the results you desire, though again the material will be mailed slowly.

An alternative appeal might be written concerning someone who is of no current interest because the files are twenty-five or thirty years old or older. In such a case I might write:

"Normally I would be understanding if an FOIA request such as my number [give the code again] was turned down for reasons of national security. However, as you know, [Subject's Name] died thirty years ago. There is nothing with which he/she was involved that could in any way affect the national security. Thus to withhold such files is to violate both the spirit and the letter of the Freedom of Information Act. As a result, I request that you send the files to me at your earliest convenience."

However you handle it, be certain that your letter is courteous, understanding, carefully reasoned, and, as much as possible, something with which no one can effectively argue. Making FOIA requests can be frustrating and time-consuming. The reactions may be petty. But the results can be a world of information concerning the subject and the people around the subject that will help give your biography greater strength than you ever thought possible.

Living Witnesses

One key to someone's character will come through the eyes of the people around your subject. You must think logically about whom you should interview.

For example, if someone is a business executive, you will want to talk with co-workers, especially underlings who may have seen both the best and the worst of the person. You should also talk with competitors in the same field, as well as people with whom he or she has done business. Other sources of information will include the members of any religious group where the person is/was affiliated, any clubs or organizations, and even the staff at favorite restaurants, bars, lounges, etc.

For actors, you not only talk with other performers who worked with the subject, you also talk with technicians, agents, publicists, and others connected with the film industry, television, and/or the theater. Again you look to clubs, religious group affiliations, and similar organizations.

It is important to talk with as many people as possible, even though some will turn you down and others will discourage you. When attempting to learn about police procedures during the serial killings that came to be called the Hillside Strangler murders, I found that there were several five-man teams. Sometimes several of the team members would talk with me. Most of the time, though, four out of the five informed me that I either wanted confidential information, they were going to write their own books after retirement in two or three years, or they did not wish to talk with a writer who had no intention of paying them.

At first I was discouraged. Then, when I saw a pattern, I realized how to play the game. I approached each police officer individually, contacting him when he was away from the team. Four of the five would refuse to talk. The fifth would say something to the effect of, "I'm glad you didn't come to me when my partners were around. They're planning to write their own book and we're supposed to have a pact that none of us will talk unless we all do it for money. That's bullshit bar talk. We're not going to write a book, and if we do, it's going to be so far in the future that your book isn't going to affect us one way or another. You've been straight about what you're trying to do. You seem to be objective. I'll talk to you in private, but don't tell the others and, if anybody asks me, I'll lie and say I refused to talk with you." Oddly, once we established the ground rules they wanted, each man, without exception, picked up the lapel microphone (see chapter six—"Interviews") I handed him, attached it to his shirt, and let me record what was said. They all trusted me to not quote them by name in the book. They also respected the recorder as my way of assuring accuracy. Thus it is important to not be discouraged.

Newspaper Research

Newspapers may be the least accurate and most needed resources for the biographer. They are inaccurate for many reasons.

First, there is no law that states that newspapers have to be factual. The First Amendment of the Constitution, as written, assures that we can publish anything we want, true or not. There are no restrictions as written, nor any restrictions by interpretation. However, there are civil penalties for publishing false information, obscene material, and similar items. These range from libel laws to laws meant to protect children from exploitation and most have such harsh penalties that reporters and editors try to be factual. This is not a legal requirement, though, and there are numerous cases throughout American history where the news has been deliberately misrepresented or presented in a one-sided manner by an editor or reporter.

Second, sources can lie or information can be hidden when the newspaper goes to press. A newspaper reporter presents what is known each day. There is no time and little space to go back and study old stories, clarifying whatever might be wrong or showing where someone lied. Each day's news is supposed to present whatever is known, yet the researcher has no continuity. You have no idea when you read the microfilm version of the *New York Times* for January 15, 1897, whether or not the story will have been found to be incorrect on March 30, 1898. You are studying one period of time, not everything that came before or comes afterwards.

Third, there can be political bias in the editing process. When I worked for one major newspaper, we reporters were sent out to objectively cover all the news, including stories that had slants we knew went against the bias of the publisher. We worked hard, wrote diligently, tried to be factual. Then, to our "surprise," there was never enough space to publish articles showing both sides. Instead only the side that revealed the publisher's bias was printed.

Fourth, there can be accidental mistakes, the most common type. For example, suppose a reporter writes a long, objective, factual article. Then, when the copyeditor is fitting it into the available space, a late-breaking story of greater importance occurs. The original article has to be cut by several paragraphs.

The copyeditor looks around desperately for the reporter who is the best person to rewrite the story to a shorter length. The reporter can assure the accuracy and objectivity needed. Unfortunately the reporter is out covering another story, a fact that forces the copyeditor to handle the rewrite personally.

The copyeditor makes every effort to be factual, but the copyeditor does not have all the information the reporter gathered, just the information used for the article. Thus there is a chance that the rewritten article will no longer be so factually correct. It is an accidental oversight, but it also keeps the newspaper from being an accurate source of historic information.

Newspapers do have value, though. Sometimes they are the only record of an event. In all cases, they give a flavor of the community, what the people felt was important, the prices for merchandise, the types of jobs available, and similar details. However, when seeking facts, they should lead you to other research whenever possible, not be considered an end in themselves.

All state historical societies recognize the value of newspapers for research. They will have several and, at times, all of the newspapers in your state on microfilm. In addition, there are central newspaper microfilm resources to which your library can refer you.

Magazines

Magazines have fewer problems than newspapers when it comes to accidental misrepresentation because they are unlikely to have late-breaking stories. However, this does not make them any more accurate for the reasons mentioned.

Sources for magazines are more difficult to find. There are central microfilm repositories and many libraries, both public and university, retain bound back issues of a wide variety of publications. These will range from such standards as *Life, Look, Colliers,* and the *Saturday Evening Post* to technical journals. You may also be able to obtain sources for back issues by contacting the publisher or the publishing company that owned a particular journal during the period when you need to study it.

Books

There is a tendency to trust a book. We all feel that anything in print and bound between covers is accurate. After all, how else would it get published?

Fortunately this statement is more likely to be true than not. Most books are as accurate as the author can make them. But authors are limited in their research sources and even books should not be considered the only source for information if other records are available.

In addition to books that might relate directly to a subject and the times, there are those that are indirectly connected to your research. For example, in working on a biography on the Swedish diplomat Folke Bernadotte who saved more than thirty thousand people from Nazi concentration camps during World War II before being murdered by the Stern Gang, I found that I gained tremendous information from books that seemed to be little related. I would find a history of Palestine, then look up Bernadotte, who was killed shortly after Israel became a nation. At first, if he was not listed, I would put the book back on the library shelf and look at others. Then I realized that there were several plotters against Bernadotte whose early lives I had been unable to flesh out. I returned to these same histories and found that one or more of the plotters' names would periodically be listed. Sometimes the name would appear as that of a messenger for some secret group fifteen years before the period where my biography began. At other times I would learn something else. By carefully reading the index, I was able to gain new insight into otherwise obscure lives.

In addition to the index, the bibliography proved a tremendous help. The bibliography led me to archives, collections of papers, diaries held in museums, and other resources I never realized existed.

Once you have identified the resources you will need and the places you will have to go, you can begin the book. Keep in mind that materials you need for the writing, including books you may have to purchase instead of borrowing from the library, are all tax deductible. Likewise, should you need to travel for an interview or even to study a location where you must be present, this is also deductible. Even telephone bills for interviews are deductible expenses. This means keeping copies of all bills you have paid and noting on each bill exactly what its purpose might be. For example, the telephone number called for an interview will be circled, then I will note the party called and the name of the book I am writing for which I conducted the interview. When I am out of town doing research, I note on each restaurant receipt the date, the city, and the book project I am researching (not all restaurant receipts list the date or even the name and location of the restaurant so this is important). I also keep a yearly desk diary for all appointments, noting all travel, to additionally confirm where I was when making the deduction. These receipts, filed by month and year, must be saved at least seven years after you have taken the deductions in case your returns are audited. And now with your resources identified, interviews, if any, planned, and your records under control, it is time to begin.

FIVE

Library Research

There are differing attitudes toward library research. While this is obviously the primary source for information with historical works, contemporary subjects usually require greater depth, such as the interviews discussed in the previous chapter. The one exception often comes with children's books. Some are written in the same manner as those for adults but others come straight from the libraries.

Mark Sufrin is a Manhattan-based biographer of numerous children's books about both the living and the dead. He has profiled President George Bush, President Harry Truman, Israel's Prime Minister Menachem Begin, and numerous other figures in fields ranging from sports to politics to art. "I must confess that I almost never, because I don't get high prices ... I mean, I take quick assignments ... I almost never use original sources. I mean, I depend upon other people's research. But, when I do somebody, I get just about everything ever written on them. Even for, like those things I did on Mussolini and the other four, Truman, Begin, etc., those were not long because they were sort of half-photographs. They were for young adults. But even then, I researched there as well as I researched a longer book."

The problem with staying in the library for researching occurs when there are seemingly contradictory sources. Books written at different times have different resources available to the author. In writing about one aspect of President Teddy Roosevelt's life, for example, I came across a period when he arranged for a new twenty-dollar gold piece to be minted without the words "In God We Trust" on it. This does not seem like much of a problem. The motto had been used on coins starting with the end of the Civil War, but it was there by chance, not by law. When Roosevelt had it removed from the new design, the assumption was made that he was either an atheist or that he wanted a firm separation of church and state. What was not expected was a backlash from the religious community that threatened him with removal from office until the motto was restored by law.

Those two assumptions were the accepted "facts" on which all writing about the incident was based for many years. Even today, almost all books dealing with his life and times stress this conclusion. But many years later, in an auction catalog published by rare coin dealer Q. David Bowers, an original Roosevelt letter was offered for sale. The letter had been held privately and is again being held privately as a result of the sale. Only through the catalog's reproduction of the letter was the truth known, because the letter, one from Roosevelt to a friend, explained his hostility to the motto. Roosevelt told how he felt it was sacrilegious, that it seemed, in his mind, to make the coin into an item of worship. He saw it almost as a false idol and it disturbed some deeply felt religious beliefs.

Suddenly an entirely different Roosevelt emerged. I quoted the letter in a biographical study of Roosevelt that I was writing, making the new information more readily available than it had been. Thus future biographers will have another tool so that a more accurate picture of Roosevelt can be depicted.

Another problem is that some biographers become lazy or "creative." Sometimes they do not adequately cross-check their sources. At other times they outright lie.

For example, there was an art dealer in the Southwest who was known for his scholarship concerning western artists. He obtained extensive research files, then turned the material over to others to "ghost" biographies in his name that would tell the stories of both famous and obscure artists of great merit. These would be artists about whom little had been written in the past. Thus his work became a primary resource.

There was one western artist whose work was so brilliant and so widely known that it was a surprise that no one had ever profiled the man. The art dealer decided to do so, arranging with a researcher to do extensive work until everything about the man that had survived, from letters to sketchbooks to paintings, had been carefully obtained, photographed, and/or studied firsthand. Then, again using a ghostwriter, the art dealer had a massive book prepared under his own name.

The book was perfectly accurate so far as anyone knew. Some of the stories were exciting, but some of the stories seemed to drag on. This was not because the writer was not skilled. This was because so much of the artist's life was spent painting, not having adventures, and working with paint and canvas is not exciting enough to try and dramatize more than once. As a result, the art dealer simply inserted stories he thought would be fun to include whenever the felt the book starting to drag. None of the stories were true, but he felt that the book became more exciting to read. Thus what has become the only resource is also a fraud in enough parts that the book cannot be considered a work of nonfiction.

Because of problems like this, Sufrin commented, "I'll tell you how by referring to the way I handle, say, specific battles of Jesse James' forays. I would get all the material and, knowing something about how fast a man can ride a horse or how fast a destroyer squadron could come up . . . You know, there would be differing times and different directions and so forth. I would piece it together. When I find something, like for instance on Catlin [Sufrin was referring to his biography of artist George Catlin, 1796-1872, one of the early painters of the American West], I sort of shift it around to make it sort of logical from what I know the run of his life would have provided."

This is not to say that facts can be changed or that fiction that sounds logical can be presented as factual. Some writers believe in telling the literal information known. If there are six different dates given for an event by six equally reliable sources, five are obviously wrong. The literal writer will quote all six, explaining that the exact date is uncertain because of the discrepancies. Other writers, still trying to be factual, will take all the dates, look at the event, try to determine any other information that might be relevant, then present one date to the reader, a date that is an educated guess. Neither approach is considered a bad one so long as careful research is involved in reaching the conclusion.

A contrasting situation might be a book on Jesus. Most nonhistorians assume that Jesus was born on December 25 because that is when Christmas is celebrated. The truth is that Jesus was born earlier in the year, perhaps in October, based on the information concerning the census being taken and other details that more carefully pinpoint the time. The December date was chosen to bring a festival of happiness to an otherwise dreary period near the winter solstice, a pagan holiday period. Anyone who studies the passages in the gospels, then relates them to Roman history and Jewish holidays of the time (approximately 4 B.C., not 1 A.D. as might be assumed) will come closer to the truth. Thus the more research you do, the more careful you are, the closer you will come to the truth. Some will guess based on their research, presenting that guess as the only option. Others will state the varying possibilities and the reasons why. What matters is that both approaches go from the best available knowledge.

"I don't think I've ever been caught on printing something fallacious," Sufrin continued. "I'm very careful about that. I usually know enough about the subject before, which is why I'm interested in them. For instance, if I get some kind of cheesy books on Harry Truman, one of these slim, bad things, I just won't use it. There may be one line that his wife said to him one day that I might or might not accept it.

"Also, I have a very good ear for what different kinds of people say. And if they say Woodrow Wilson said, 'Hey, baby ...' I mean ...

"Usually a lazy writer will say, 'after three years of exhibiting at Egyptian Hall ...' Whereas a guy who works at the Smithsonian who did the introduction to a book on the Indian gallery will say, 'he didn't renew his lease for the third year.' And then I follow his career for the next couple of years and I say, 'Aha! He didn't renew his lease for the third year. He came back and renewed it for six months, but that was after his tour of the provinces.'

"So you can generally get quite a good sense of it by puzzling it out. I was generally so good about doing battles or combat stuff, I once got a letter from a Philippine scout who served in the Philippines and told me I must have been there at that battle. I wasn't at that battle. I knew enough about the war, even if I hadn't been there, I knew enough about the war to know what happened. And very often I've gotten things like, 'this is the first time we've ever had a correct account of such and such.'

"I think most writers, even good military writers, are careless."

Sufrin maintains an extensive library related to World War II, approximately one thousand books at hand at all times. "When I was doing so much writing about the period, I got to be known at what they call the book and magazine branches of the various [armed] services. And they would send me service records, send me battle reports that weren't classified. I could get whatever I wanted. But there's been so much [written] on it that there's really no need, except when I needed a guy's service record to see exactly what he did.

"Even when I did this kids' biography on Bush, I got his service record to make it accurate. I just called the Navy here and they put me on to somebody in Washington." The service records are considered public information and available to anyone.

"The thing to do is always ask for the public relations people. They're always desperate to have their name in books and magazines, and they're very helpful. Of course, the guy will always say, 'Warrant Officer Jones.' And you say 'My name is Mark Sufrin.'

" 'Yes, sir. I'll have that for you, sir, as soon as possible, sir.' They're very deferential."

Sufrin does do interviews at times, though. If there might be living relatives or acquaintances of the people about whom he is writing, he has, at times, placed advertisements in the *New York Times* classified section. He states that he is writing a book and seeking people who knew his subject. Then, as he talks with one, he gains referrals to others.

Sufrin will also use specialized libraries in other parts of the state or other parts of the country. However, because young adult books do not pay large advances, he seldom is able to travel to any great degree, further forcing his use of libraries.

Interlibrary Loans

Most library systems offer what are known as interlibrary loans. If the book(s) you seek is not in one library, a search can be instituted in various ways. Some libraries will search only among their branches. Others will look throughout their state system. And a few will search anywhere in the country. There may be no charge for the service, there may be a small fee, or there may be a fee plus costs such as insurance for a rare, though still circulating volume.

Specialty Libraries

Among the most important repositories available to the general public for research are the Library of Congress, a respository of every book ever written in the United States, and the National Archives, both in Washington, D.C. The National Archives has everything from ship manifests to the personal papers of all manner of individuals.

University libraries often are excellent resources for historical material. The vast majority of such libraries are open to the general public with special permission from the library director. Some university libraries will allow nonstudents to remove books. Almost all will let you do research within the library itself so long as you remove nothing from the facility. Since they tend to keep extremely long hours as a service for the students, these can be an excellent help with your research.

Reference Librarians

Most larger libraries have one or more library-trained reference librarians along with various paid staff members and volunteers. Talk with the professionals, explain what person or era you are researching, and you are likely to gain far more assistance than you realize. Their jobs require them to know how to find the obscure and the little known, as well as the references available to locate material in other facilities. They can save you tremendous amounts of research time if you talk with them at the start.

Newspaper Collections

Newspapers are an excellent source of information, though not always an accurate one. Yet despite occasional lapses, more common during the early years of this century than they are today, newspapers provide extensive firsthand information. Names, dates, quotes, eyewitness accounts, and similar information are available. You also develop a sense of the times and the things the people valued through the columns, the editorials, the advertisements, and even the cartoons.

Most public libraries and many university facilities retain extensive holdings of newspapers. At the very least they are likely to have the *New York Times* on microfilm, the papers dating back a century or longer. Most will also retain the local newspaper and, where it is different, whatever paper is the largest in your particular state. They will also usually have the *New York Times* index in which you can check names and subjects. Some state and local papers will also be indexed, but most are not. The process is too tedious and expensive.

State historical societies usually have every newspaper published within the state that has been either stored on microfilm (or, in some instances, microfiche) or collected whole. The problem with the latter is that newspapers have a high acid content such that, the older they get, the more likely they are to disintegrate when handled. Thus older papers may not be available for research even if they are in the collection.

Diaries

Many universities and historical societies, as well as some public libraries, will have diaries and collections of personal papers donated to them or copies of privately published diaries where a few dozen or even a few hundred copies were printed for limited distribution. Again these are excellent resources to help you with your biography though they need to be taken cautiously.

Diaries are considered primary resources by writers because they were written by the person about whom they are writing. However, this does not mean that they are accurate. Most diarists have a sense that their work will be read by others, or at least they hope that this will be the case. While some believe in scrupulous honesty and accuracy, others lie. They present their lives in either a positive manner or they downplay the negative, ideally leaving the impression that they were victims of whatever went wrong.

Does this mean that you should avoid using them? Quite the contrary. Even where they are inaccurate they have great value because they indicate the way the subject wished to be remembered by others. Thus they are windows to that person's attitude about him or her self and life. They also frequently provide a chronology of events in the diarist's life that help you research other information that you need.

Other Library Tips

Larger libraries may have closed stacks, areas where older and less popular books are stored. An open stack allows anyone to explore the entire holding. A closed stack requires you to request a specific volume. However, if you talk with the head librarian, explaining the research that you are doing, you will often be allowed to explore the books yourself. This can be extremely important because often your subject is too obscure to be the subject of a book. Instead, his or her name is found in the index of books about others during the time that your subject lived. Being able to thumb through the indexes of other books may provide you with information you otherwise could not find.

Check to see if the library has a typewriter you can use or if you can bring in either a portable typewriter or computer for working. I carry a laptop with me when going over reference materials, typing out notes so that I am more productive than taking notes in longhand. Some libraries will let you use a typewriter or take a book to a typing room where you can make the notes. You may also find that carrying a portable tape recorder and reading aloud will be faster than longhand during your research. These are also less expensive than making photocopies. Just be certain to record the name of the book, publisher, and related bibliographic information you will need to include in your final work.

University libraries and some public libraries maintain a collection of doctoral dissertations. Often these contain in-depth research on a particular subject that will directly relate to the biography that you are doing. In theory these papers are screened by experts before the student is awarded a doctoral degree and thus the material is quite valuable. In practice the accuracy must be questioned because cross-checking is not always so complete as you might think. Students have been known to create "facts" to enhance a paper, to plagiarize, and to make mistakes, all of which occasionally go unnoticed by the review committee. It is better to take such papers as guides, checking the information and using the material to, perhaps, send you in a different direction than you have been, than to assume that it is completely accurate.

Finally, keep in mind that travel to libraries can be tax deductible. If you live in a small community and need to travel to a major university, historical society, and/or major city library, all expenses will be legitimate business deductions provided your stay and activities are all related to your research. For example, I have arranged to work in the New York Public Library, the library of the New York State Historical Society, and the library of the Museum of Modern Art for a biography I am writing. So long as I spend the hours these facilities are open researching my project, I can deduct the flight, the hotel, and a reasonable amount for meals (no expensive wines or going to the fanciest restaurants in the city). I can also choose to relax at shows and concerts (the prices for which are not deductible) in the evenings, taking a minivacation while legitimately completing my work. Just be certain to keep receipts for everything deductible, noting the project you are researching on the receipts as further proof of the reason for your trip.

SIX

Conducting Interviews

> I love the breathtaking way we walk into people's lives and
> ask them anything we want and then leave. For a moment
> you have available to you the whole universe of a person's
> life — the pain and the suffering and the joy and the strug-
> gle. You can learn from it and take it with you, and then
> come back the next day with somebody else. That's what I
> like to do.
>
> — Diane Sawyer
> quoted by Richard Zoglin in
> *Time* magazine, August 7, 1989.

I like to tell students that the wonderful part about feature writing is that we get paid for being nosey. We can ask anyone anything
and no one is offended. They may not respond; they may say that
what we have asked is none of our business. But they are not offended that we have chosen to ask the questions involved and, in
most instances, they will respond to some degree.

Writing a biography is quite different from the type of broadcast
journalism ABC News' Diane Sawyer was describing and, frequently, from the type of skills needed for feature writing. First
there is the time factor. We are not seeking a simple answer or the
surface emotion, the types of responses most likely encountered
with shorter material and/or immediate deadlines. We need to look
below the surface, to discover the depth within. This means different skills, different approaches.

The As-Told-To Autobiography

An as-told-to autobiography creates the most intimate writing relationship it is possible to experience. You, the writer, have to know
almost everything about an individual, no matter how intimate the
details. You literally have to know someone better than his or her
spouse or lover. You need to understand not only the individual's
actions and experiences that led to the person's being a good subject, you also have to understand the reasons behind what happened. You will come to know the pleasure, the pain, and the dirty

little secrets that all of us like to wall off in a mental closet and not have to think about again. This is your job, your burden, your delight.

Before you start asking questions, some writers feel that you should understand the subject's motive for writing the book. I, personally, have never cared so long as the person is willing to be truthful and that I can be comfortable with the fact that nothing has gone into the book that is inaccurate.

Motives vary, of course. Henry Hawksworth was the first male multiple personality ever to gain national recognition in the United States. He had just finished therapy and wanted to review his life before getting on with more important things than being a former dissociating hysteric as his illness was more formally known.

"Leo Janus, who collaborated with Chuck Yeager on his book, said to me that you have to find out why the person who's doing this book wants to do the book," said Ken Turan. "When you find that out, you'll know the kind of book you're going to end up with.

"Patty Duke really wanted to clear the decks. She wanted to get everything out. She wanted to tell her story, to clear up all of the rumors, clear up all the innuendoes about earlier in her life." It was a time of reflection, of looking back and getting ready for the next forty years of her life.

As a writer, no matter what the motive may be, it is still your job to be thorough and accurate.

Planning Time

During the early stages of interviewing, neither you nor your subject has any idea how long it will take. You both must be willing to commit to far more hours than you anticipate at first. You also must be willing to explore the right way to work for your subject. For example, when working with actress Patty Duke, Ken Turan said:

"I did go on location with her for a week at the very beginning because she thought she'd have a lot of time. As it turned out, we got some very good work done, but her time was not as good as we thought it might be. So we stopped. We didn't do that. She didn't have to go on location again, but even if she had, I don't think I would have gone because I don't think that's an ideal situation.

"What I found was ideal was to meet with her two, possibly three times a week for a couple hours at a time. Emotionally and just energy-wise, it's intense. You're trying to think and drag things out and come up with things. It's a lot of mental work and her stuff was even harder because it was very emotional. But anybody, past two hours, starts to drag. It wasn't a hard fact. Sometimes we'd go two-and-a-half or a little longer if things were really going well. But I can't imagine going more than three hours."

Equipment for the Interview

Life was much simpler when notes were made with a quill pen. There were no choices when you wanted to write. Everything was printed or in longhand.

The typewriter made work go faster when writing, but few people ever took notes with such a machine, and fewer still take notes with the laptop computer. Although I carry a notebook and pen, I might as well be using the quill. There are too many times when the subject must be stopped while you make a detailed quote. In the course of an article interview there are no problems. When it comes to the notes for a book, there are plenty of times when your hand will cramp and the words will seem to trail off the page as you lose the ability to concentrate. An interview is a catharsis for the subject. It is an often boring task for you, no matter how exciting the book ultimately becomes.

My answer for book interviews is to use a tape recorder. This is a surprisingly controversial approach among many biographers. Typically they claim that a tape recorder is an intruder that makes their subjects uncomfortable. This may be the case for the first few moments, but after conducting hundreds of interviews with such machines, I would not be without them.

Why Tape Record?

There are several reasons for tape recording interviews, the most critical one being accuracy. Kitty Kelley is one of the most controversial unauthorized biographers of our day. She has profiled such famous names as Elizabeth Taylor, Jacqueline Kennedy Onassis, Frank Sinatra, and Nancy Reagan. Her subjects rarely will talk with her, many, such as Frank Sinatra, threatening to sue her. Her skill comes from interviewing the people who knew the subjects, who grew up with them, worked with or for them. She talks with everyone who has any connection with the subject, then develops a profile of the individual from the evidence she has documented in this way. While her work is supplemented with published materials, FOIA papers, and other items, the interviews are of the greatest concern.

For example, Kitty Kelley arranged to interview Peter Lawford during her research for the Frank Sinatra book. She met Peter at his home, accompanied by a photographer who frequently did work for *Life* magazine. Peter had been a part of what was known as the "clan" and frequently called the "rat pack," a group of friends that included Lawford, Sinatra, comedian Joey Bishop, entertainer Sammy Davis, Jr., and singer Dean Martin. He was also an alcoholic and drug addict who would be dead in a few months.

Patricia Seaton, the woman who lived with Peter and became his last wife, arrived home in the midst of the interview, something she had not known Peter had agreed to do. She became irate with Kelley, insisting that Kitty was there under false pretenses, allegedly tricking Peter into thinking the interview was to be about himself for *Life*, not about Sinatra. Peter had had a turbulent relationship with Sinatra and Patricia felt that Lawford would not have voluntarily given an interview for the book.

Later there was talk of a lawsuit against Kelley for, among other things, misrepresenting herself. However, because she tape recorded the entire session with Lawford, she felt that she would triumph. She said that the tape cleared her of all charges that she misrepresented why she was there and what she was doing. The fact that the lawsuit never came about speaks strongly for her statement. Certainly the tape assured that the truth would be known.

Not every book requires interviews that could lead to lawsuits, of course. The number of biographies where libel issues are a concern is minimal. But accuracy is always a problem and it is easy to miss something when making notes during hour after hour of interviewing. In addition, the tape recordings help you retain the tone and style of speech of the people you interview. Being able to capture their exact words and phrases when quoting them helps make your book come alive.

"I think a tape recording is essential," said Ken Turan. "I think it's much harder to get the tiny nuances of speech that characterize a person, that give a person individuality, without using a tape recorder. It's not impossible, but I think it's much harder."

This does not mean that you should not use a notebook. I always work with one for several reasons, the most important of which is because I could have mechanical failure of my equipment and the notebook assures that will not be a problem (yes, I carry an extra pen and refill). I can also note important parts of what I am hearing, putting down the tape number (I number them consecutively), the side, and approximately how far into the recording I might be. You can also use the counter that comes with most cassette recorders, but the numbers are not consistent from machine to machine. I prefer noting that I am approximately one-third into the tape, one-fourth into it, or whatever.

Other Concerns

Ted's Law of Writing Tools states that all equipment we use—pens, tape recorders, microphones, and batteries—is subject to intimidation. So long as an item thinks it is irreplaceable, it will die, be lost, or commit suicide. I have had fresh batteries that tested flawlessly suddenly stop working ten minutes into an interview because I realized I had no spares. Likewise, I have had the ink in fresh pen refills suddenly clot and jam the point the moment it realized I had left my spare in the car. By contrast, when I carry far more supplies than I should need — extra batteries, a spare pen plus a refill, etc. — the equipment works seemingly forever. One microphone battery normally lasts twenty-one hours. Yet during one series of interviews I had three spares in my briefcase and, when I checked the volume of tape I had recorded, I discovered that it had been working almost fifty hours and was still going strong. Thus spares are critical, if only for intimidation purposes.

Telephone Tape Recording

There is more controversy and nonsense about tape recording on the telephone than for any other subject. Some telephone directories in a few cities even have a note stating that there is a telephone company "tariff" against recording over the phone without all parties being aware. But this "tariff" is meaningless in all cases, sometimes meant to intimidate you into buying an approved recorder that generates a tone every few seconds, in other instances.

Truth: Under Federal law and the laws of almost half the states, it is perfectly legal to record over the telephone without telling the person with whom you are talking that you are recording. You may not wiretap, but there are three devices that are perfectly proper to use.

The most expensive device is one sold by Radio Shack and a few other companies for a price that ranges from twenty to thirty dollars, depending upon the manufacturer and retailer. One end plugs into a standard wall jack such as you find with all contemporary modular telephones. Then you plug your telephone into a jack that is in a small control box at the end of the cord. A wire comes from the other side and leads to two plugs, one meant to go into the external microphone jack (an inexpensive adapter plug will be needed for some machines) of any tape recorder and the other, a smaller one, meant to go into the remote control slot found in many tape recorders. You do not have to have a remote control slot, nor do you have to use one when you do. All that matters is that the one end is plugged directly into the microphone slot.

The box has a switch attached to it allowing you to rig the unit to record every time the telephone is picked up or to just play the recorder. I ignore the switch, leaving it just on "record," and leave the tape recorder plugged in but turned off. I set the tape recorder to record as I would if using it manually when I need to record an interview. But no matter how you feel you want to use yours, this is simple to operate and the sound quality is equal to or better than what you will hear when you listen to the telephone receiver.

The second device is called an "O" ring. It is a circular device that slides over the ear piece of a standard table model telephone. It will not fit on princess type telephones or other designs. However, it will work with pay telephones and can be used when calling from a public area. One end slips around the earpiece and then it is attached by a cord to the tape recorder's microphone slot. Except for fitting around the earpiece, it is the same as an external microphone in the way it is handled by the tape recorder. The cost is under five dollars, though these are not so readily found. I have purchased mine from the Calrad Corporation in California, a company that sells its products to a number of independent and small chain electronic stores. I have not seen it carried by the larger chains, though, so I usually buy several at a time when I need them.

The most common inexpensive device is the induction coil. There are different types, the most frequently seen being attached to a suction cup. You place the suction cup against the earpiece and plug the other end into your tape recorder, again just as you would an external microphone. A variation has a metal plate that fits underneath the telephone, but the concept is the same. Sometimes these devices work well and sometimes they work quite poorly. If you plan to buy one and the store manager will let you, try it in the store to be certain it will work for you. These are also poorly constructed and relatively easily broken so always carry a spare.

Once you have your telephone recording device, call your state's attorney general's office and ask if such recording is legal in your state. Be certain the attorney with whom you talk checks the law books because I have found that most attorneys "know" it is illegal until they check the records. Then they are shocked to learn that it is perfectly proper, at least in approximately half the states.

Should you be in a state where such recording is illegal, you can still do it. However, early on in the conversation you are expected to say, on tape, that you are recording and get the subject's permission to do so. There are exceptions, such as in California where you do not have to alert the subject if the subject you are recording is trying to extort you and you are trying to prove the extortion with the tape recording. But such exceptions will not affect you as an interviewer.

Likewise, it is legal to telephone a state where recordings cannot be made without alerting the subject and not tell the person you are recording the conversation. For example, I live in Ohio where it is legal to make tape recordings by telephone. I often call California where such recordings are not legal, making tape recordings when necessary. I do not have to tell the person I am making the recording even though, if I lived in California and called Ohio, I would have to alert the subject in Ohio to what I was doing in order to comply with the California law.

I do not make tapes of all my telephone calls when working on a biography or any other writing project. This would be needlessly expensive. However, I do make tapes when working on highly technical matters, using the telephone for interviews in place of person-to-person meetings (the calls often run one to two hours in length during such times), and when checking statements that are potentially libelous.

Virgin Tapes

The only other important point to know about telephone tape recording is how you have to handle it in order for it to be legal in a court of law. Actually, this is the case with all tape recording because tapes can be electronically doctored.

In order for a tape to be considered admissible as evidence in court, it must be a virgin tape that is used only once. Each time it is erased, either with a bulk eraser that erases the entire tape or by recording over what has been recorded, there is electronic evidence that can be detected by special instruments. The fact is that you may be reusing an older tape for convenience and cost effectiveness, the new recording made honestly and without change. But the act of rerecording will result in your potentially being accused of doctoring the material. It must not be done.

To protect the tape from accidental reuse, you will notice that there are two tabs on a standard cassette, the tabs on the end exactly opposite where the tape path is visible. These come against a probe that is on all cassette recorders. When you push the record button the probe touches the tabs and the machine will record. If you punch out the tabs (I use the tip of a pen to punch them), the probe goes into a slight hollow and prevents recording, though the tape will play normally. In fact, all commercially prerecorded tapes have the tabs removed so you cannot accidentally erase the music or other information. Should you ever want to reuse the tapes for recording nonessential material, you just take a small piece of adhesive tape and cover the hole. The adhesive tape acts just like the tab and allows the cassette to be recorded again.

Microcassettes have the tabs on the narrow sides instead of directly opposite the tape path. They are smaller, a little harder to spot, but function in the same manner.

Transcribing Tape

The one concern most writers overlook until too late is what you do with tapes after you have made them. Transcribing a recording is not an easy task, as any professional typist can tell you. There are many devices available to help you, ranging from separate transcribing machines to start/stop foot pedals that attach to any tape recorder with a remote jack built into the unit. However, trying to listen intently so that you transcribe the exact words is both difficult and rather slow. Most professional typists anticipate having to work on a three-to-one ratio. This means that for every hour of tape, they will be transcribing for three hours.

There are exceptions, of course. I have been working with a Tucson, Arizona, transcriber who is the fastest, most effective typist I have ever encountered. She has worked with me for well over ten years and I would not want to have to consider replacing her. She can transcribe an hour tape in an hour, a skill that is rare to find.

If you transcribe your own work, you are going to be wasting much of your time. It is a tedious process that I feel the writer should avoid if possible. You can always play back a portion of the tape to get a feel for the voice and the nuances of the character. But most of the time you will be looking for quotes and these are most easily obtained by skimming through the transcription of the tape.

My advice is to find the fastest, most accurate, and least expensive transcriber you can locate in your area. Then use the individual based on your advance. If you receive enough of an advance (explained later in this book) to be able to afford the transcriber, doing it yourself is false economy. If the advance is either too small or you do not receive any money up front, then you may only be able to afford to transcribe the material yourself. But given the choice, you will find that you are most productive when someone else handles this tedious though essential chore.

Interviewing the Primary Subject

There are many ways to work when interviewing the subject of your authorized biography or as-told-to autobiography. Bill Novak is able to take notes as rapidly as the person speaks and feels that a tape recorder only makes his subjects uncomfortable. Toward the end of their time working together, he brings a laptop computer to the interview sessions and types as they speak. He is an unusually rapid, skilled typist who can work as fast as they speak and is able to type as he looks at them. This is a rare talent and not one most of us could emulate.

Some writers use only tape recording, though I always feel that there is a risk of an unexpected mechanical problem that will cause me to lose critical material. My preference is one chosen by most biographers whom I have interviewed. I tape record and take notes as described earlier.

Setting the Scene

You are not important when working with your subject. You are a means to an end. The subject must be comfortable with you and this means adjusting to his or her needs. If you are freshest during the early hours of the morning and your subject likes to work at midnight, then you will conduct your interviews at midnight. Likewise, if you hate cigarette smoke and your subject relaxes by chain smoking, then you will breathe foul air without complaint, taking long walks to clear your lungs a bit when you are not in session. Your job is to get the material regardless of what it takes.

Sometimes the interview situation can be humorous. Television star Angie Dickinson is known for having the most glamorous legs in Hollywood. She is now of an age where many other actresses are considered "matronly," yet she remains extremely beautiful. She also was an intimate of John Kennedy and Peter Lawford whom I needed to interview when working on the Peter Lawford story. Patricia S. Lawford arranged the interview at Angie's house and came along with me to talk with the star. What neither of us realized was that Angie would be slightly uncomfortable with another woman in her living room.

Immediately after we arrived, Angie rearranged the chairs so that I was positioned so I could look at her and only at her. Patricia was placed behind me and to the side in such a way that I could barely see her with my peripheral vision. I would only be comfortable looking directly at Angie, even if Patricia said something. Then Angie sat in such a way that she alternately looked directly at me or down at Patricia's legs, her eyes following a very obvious path. It was rather humorous, but it made her more comfortable during the interview and that was what mattered.

You will also find that you sometimes touch nerves that you do not expect when conducting the interviews. Your subject may need to get away from you, become ill at the thought and need to take time off, or otherwise react. Again, you must adapt.

The biographers interviewed for this book primarily had few problems. Their subjects treated the sessions like a job, devoting a set number of hours per day or per week to the task. Everything was businesslike and there were few problems.

I have seldom been that lucky. When I wrote the authorized biography of artist Arnold Friberg, he was living in emotional hell.

His beloved wife was dying of all manner of illnesses and her mind had been so seriously affected that she was no longer a rational person. I worked with him during a period when she lost all sense of lucidity and the shock took a tremendous toll on him. For example, we went to see her in the nursing home, Arnold taking a new painting to show her. She looked at it and began commenting with an expert's eye, her statements insightful and his pride in her understanding and knowledge making him beam with delight. Then, in midsentence, her mind stopped functioning rationally and she began babbling about things that had nothing to do with the painting or discussion. She had no idea who I was or why I was there, and the painting seemed to disappear from her mind's eye. When we left, Arnold seemed to have doubled in age, his shoulders hunched, his face heavily lined, his gait one of someone in deep sorrow.

As his wife deteriorated, Arnold fell in love with a woman who had married a man whom she did not love but who could provide a decent father figure for her children. The two of them longed to be together, but they were both married even though one marriage was loveless and the other was destroyed by illness and a mind wasted to near nothingness. The anguish he felt seeing his wife no longer his wife and having a love with a woman who could not be his own nearly destroyed him. He spent as little time in the house he and his wife built as possible, preferring to essentially live in his studio, sleeping in a torn, battered recliner. He worked until he dropped, seldom getting more than four hours' rest a night. And in order to capture him completely, I had to maintain his pace.

John DeLorean was in the midst of legal battles when I worked with him. I took a hotel room on the fringes of Beverly Hills that was a relatively short walk to his lawyer's office, leaving each day open for whatever time we would have together. Sometimes we worked for hours, having lunch and dinner together. At other times we worked for ten minutes before being interrupted by his attorney who needed an instant conference that might last for a few minutes or a few hours. I spent much time waiting (yes, I carried other projects to work on during such periods or I read legal documents related to his cases) and occasionally tape recorded in his car or as we watched his son play soccer at his junior high school.

And when working on the story of a boy who almost died of liver disease, I had to interview doctors and nurses who no longer worked the shifts they had worked when he was in the hospital. I took a hotel room near the hospital and conducted interviews on every shift. Sometimes I worked twenty hours straight through. At other times I would take an hour or two for a nap at the hotel, then return to the hospital for the next interview. I had to work when it was convenient for the subjects.

Respecting the Subjects

No matter whom you interview, no matter what type of person he or she might be, it is always necessary to show respect. Over time you can dress in whatever way they seem most comfortable. But at the start of the relationship, a degree of formality is essential. It is a way of saying that you honor them enough to make a good appearance and, though they may laugh and tell you that you will have to learn to dress for their area, you will find that you gain their confidence faster.

My tendency, as a male, is to always wear a suit and tie in any conservative community. This means most of the East Coast and many other parts of the country. When working in extremely hot, muggy areas I substitute good slacks, a long-sleeved shirt, and a necktie for the suit. In either case, my shoes are always shined.

(Note: In case you think that I am comfortable this way, I am writing this while wearing an old T-shirt, worn Wranglers, and hiking boots that have seen a few too many miles of walking.)

Women should wear whatever is appropriate for conservative business dress in your area. This may mean a dress or a good skirt and blouse. In some areas a pants suit is also acceptable.

You should also arrive a few minutes early for your interview. You want the subject to feel that you know his or her time is important and that the person will not ever have to wait for you.

Currently much of my work involves Hollywood stars or their next of kin. I have met Robert Wagner in the clothing he wears while working on his ranch, Angie Dickinson while relaxing at her home, Jack Lemmon in his business office, Patricia Lawford in a robe and curlers, and various others in dress ranging from swimsuits to tuxedos. Most of them laughed about my being a few minutes early for our appointment—"Out here people seem to think that if you're an hour late, you're 'fashionably early,' " one star commented. "Thank God I don't have to put up with that from you." Or they laughed about my wearing a shirt and tie—"This is California, for God's sake. Nobody dresses decently out here. Come into my living room and we'll talk about it. Somebody's got to teach you what Hollywood's really like." And then they talked in-depth, intimately, and in detail. More important, these were often individuals who have not allowed an interview for years other than those required as part of the publicity for a movie or television show.

In fact, the less accustomed to respect someone might be, the more they respond to being treated that way. This is especially true with street people such as gamblers, hustlers, and prostitutes. In fact, the Los Angeles County Sheriff's Department's Homicide Unit has all its men wear the type of clothing I am describing even though they are frequently encountering what might best be called "lowlifes." They have one of the best arrest and conviction records in the country because the street people respond to their being treated with dignity, providing information they might otherwise withhold.

Beginning the Interview

There is no right way to start an interview with the subject of an authorized biography or as-told-to autobiography. Both of you are going to be a little awkward. You each are aware that there is much work ahead of you. Your subject may be a little nervous about what you expect and you may be apprehensive about some of the questions you need to ask. Fortunately you have extensive time available for the project and can talk about any area of the person's life.

Although you may not realize it, your subject has certain expectations concerning your demeanor, though these are often unspoken and, perhaps, unrecognized until you inadvertently violate them. The first and most important is that you are expected to listen to the subject. Truly listen. Looking the person in the eyes, listening not only to the specific answer to the question that you asked but to everything else the person is saying. Letting the person go off on a tangent when it is important, gently guiding the subject back to the area of concern when it is not.

Second, you must accept what you are hearing, no matter how shocking or surprising. A biographer will uncover the dirty little secrets within a family and they must be fully understood, even if you never repeat them in the book. In the course of my work, for example, I have heard stories of incest among the rich and famous, sadomasochistic sex, rape, and unconscionable violence. Sometimes the individual I am interviewing was the one who committed the acts. Sometimes the subject was the victim. And sometimes the victim grows up to do the same actions to his or her child. Yet neither my words nor my body language could in any way condemn or show my horror and/or disgust.

The reason for this is that when someone has "dirty little secrets," they have either been condemned for their actions or emotions by others or they have condemned themselves. A biographer must be accepting, noncritical, nonjudgmental. You can express emotion appropriately, but only after you have placed yourself in their position at the time the event occurred.

The difference between a good interviewer and a bad one is the ability to look at what you are being told from the viewpoint of the person who is talking. For example, there was a period when I was interviewing Ken Bianchi, the Los Angeles Hillside Strangler, when I arrived at the jail and found him depressed and withdrawn. He had murdered seventeen girls and women, raping most of them. He was acting out pain with murder, his crimes being extreme, violent ones.

There is a hierarchy in prison with the most respected men being bank robbers and police killers. The least respected, and the most likely to be brutalized or killed once they are behind bars, are child molestors and rapists, especially those who rape young children. Even the police and prison guards share such attitudes with the exception of someone who has murdered one of their own. Thus Bianchi had been subjected to quite a bit of verbal abuse at least and may have been pushed around by either guards or inmates while waiting, under a sentence already imposed, to begin testifying against his cousin who was later convicted of being an accomplice during the Los Angeles phase of a three-state murder spree.

I also knew that the only life that Bianchi valued was that of his small son, Sean. But Sean's mother, upon learning the truth about the man she loved and lived with, refused to bring Sean to the jail for a visit. Though the child was still young enough not to know what was happening to his father, his mother wanted nothing to do with Bianchi. She certainly did not want her son to grow to have any memories of his father.

The lack of his son's presence hurt Ken. This was also a man who harbored great anger toward women and had had a very disturbed childhood according to medical reports I had obtained. He was also being taken out each night by investigators, driven through the streets of Los Angeles County, and asked to show the different locations of the pickups, the rapes, the murders, and the disposing of the bodies. The work was being done in preparation for the trial of his cousin, and the investigators hated him. They were constantly verbally attacking him and he was desperate for acceptance.

Knowing all this, and needing information from him, I went into my jailhouse meeting with Bianchi and said, "You know, if I were you, I'd want Kelli [the woman he lived with] dead."

Bianchi stared at me, shocked. "What do you mean?" he asked.

"I'd want her dead," I repeated. "She's doing nothing but causing you pain by not coming to visit you and keeping you from seeing your son, Sean. If she were dead, you wouldn't have all this pain."

Suddenly Ken Bianchi's face seemed younger. He grinned, relaxed, and said, "You understand." And then he talked about his life, his feelings, his murders. I had accepted him.

Did I condone what he had done? Of course not. Did I think that Kelli should be dead? Nonsense! Kelli and I had grown close and I ached for the pain she had endured not knowing the type of monster with whom she was living. I was delighted that she refused to come by the jail and she certainly had no business bringing their four-year-old child. What I had done was accepted Ken Bianchi, accepted his pain, his rage, his method for survival. Thus I was quite comfortable with saying, "If I were you . . ." because, if I had been him, that is exactly what I would have been feeling.

Bill Novak was working with Nancy Reagan at the ranch she and her husband, former President Reagan, own in California. Novak happened to be on the grounds, near the barn, when he discovered the former president walking nearby. He felt he had to say something, though he was unnerved by his proximity to the man who for eight years was one of a handful of international leaders who held the fate of the world in their hands.

Novak explained that he looked around, then noticed an object hanging over the entrance to the barn. It was an unusual item, obviously a gift, and gave him a focus to ask the president about.

"When I got the job . . ." the President began, and his words shocked Novak. He said that he barely heard the rest of the explanation. "When I got the job . . ." He realized that Ronald Reagan looked upon his election to the presidency of the United States as a "job." It was as if there was little difference between gaining that position and winning a starring role in a movie back before he had entered politics.

Perhaps there was more to what he meant. Perhaps had Novak had more time to speak with him instead of having to work with the president's wife, Reagan would have clarified the meaning. But there was no time and the words surprised him. Yet Novak, the consummate professional, accepted them, accepted the former president, and continued working with Nancy Reagan without asking about the incident or the couple's attitude toward the White House.

Ariane Sheppard explained the problems that subjects have with their biographers. She is not a writer but was part of what was once one of the biggest stories in the United States.

Ariane was the half-sister of Magda Goebbels, wife of Hitler's propaganda minister during World War II. She frequently played with Adolf Hitler when she was growing up and may have been the last civilian to be in the bunker with Hitler and the Goebbels family before they committed suicide.

Later Ariane was married to osteopathic physician Dr. Sam Sheppard after he was released from jail for the murder of his wife, Marilyn. Sheppard had essentially been tried and convicted by newspaper reporting. Louis B. Seltzer, editor of the *Cleveland Press*, had run such headlines as "Sheppard's Guilty! Bring Him In" during the investigation. It was the 1950s, a period of highly exploitive journalism, and it took a young, unknown lawyer named F. Lee Bailey to win a new trial. The case went to the U.S. Supreme Court, made international headlines, and then resulted in the acquittal of Sheppard. Ariane, who had met him through correspondence while living in Europe, married the doctor. Then the two of them became the subject for several books and a television movie starring actor George Peppard.

Ariane was deeply hurt by the actions of the various writers involved with her story. They heard of the happy times with Hitler when she was a child (she turned sixteen two weeks after the suicides in the bunker so she was never a part of the inhumane political machine). They learned of her evacuation to a small town when the Russian soldiers moved across Germany, of her being hidden in the dark rafters of a farm house to avoid being raped and possibly murdered by the men. They also learned of her first marriage and the divorce that occurred when her husband slapped their two-year-old daughter, so brain-damaging the child that she grew to adulthood without ever advancing mentally. And always the reactions were the same. "You were where?" "You did what?" "That's shocking!" "How could you?" "How could they?" "Oh, my God!"

There was no acceptance. There was shock, disbelief, horror, and delight. "They didn't try to know me," she said. "I was badly hurt and felt that no one was interested in telling my story or understanding what I went through." And as a result, none of the writers were given more than a partial story. Ariane withheld much of the information that would have made for a far more fascinating book on the Sheppards because the interviewers caused her so much pain.

My approach is to try and recreate the circumstances of the person's life in my own mind. Everyone reacts in a logical, consistent manner to stimulus. If you go back far enough in their lives, you can begin to see the influences.

For example, for many years Jacqueline Bouvier Kennedy Onassis was questioned for having stayed with a womanizing husband. She was accused of being heartless, of seeking only his money, of being manipulative. There were also critics who decided that no woman would do what she did under any circumstances, a fact that meant the stories of the womanizing were either lies or greatly exaggerated. Only a few biographers accepted Jackie and began looking into her background, to see the influences that existed as she was growing up.

The truth proved to be that Jackie's father, "Black Jack" Bouvier, was a notorious womanizer himself. His actions were so outrageous that the night he and Jackie's mother were married, while they were literally on the first twenty-four hours of their honeymoon on board a cruise ship, he picked up another woman and slept with her. Yet her mother stayed with the man for many years, talking freely about what he had done. Thus Jackie was obviously raised in a hurting, dysfunctional family where her only marital role was one that revealed only the woman being faithful.

Jack Kennedy was raised in a somewhat similar manner. His father had a number of affairs, including one with actress Gloria Swanson, considered by many to be the greatest actress of the day. Joe Kennedy took matters a step further than "Black Jack" Bouvier. He brought Gloria and her young daughter home with him, putting the mother into her own room and having Gloria's daughter live in his daughter, Pat Kennedy's room. Not only did this influence the young Jack Kennedy, it also influenced Pat, who tolerated the womanizing of her own husband, actor Peter Lawford.

Suddenly the biographer was no longer writing about a woman who was stupid, a liar, a self-centered hedonist, a greedy individual, or any of the other names she had been called. By accepting Jackie and trying to understand what had taken place by truly researching her past, then thinking about how anyone, raised the same way, might react, a very different portrait emerged. Jackie became an obvious adult victim of child abuse, a woman wracked with painful scarring from her earliest days, who coped the only way she had learned to cope. The biographies became richer, fuller, more understandable, and far superior to those that were unable to accept the reality of what the woman had accomplished.

Breaking the Ice

Television interviewer Barbara Walters will often use the trick of asking an interview subject who is not too responsive what he or she does in a typical day. This can be an icebreaker, though it has more meaning for a short television segment than for the three hundred or four hundred or more pages you must fill with an adult biography.

Other interviewers may ask about a recent event that put the person in the news. Or they may ask about the subject's business. And some will take them back to childhood. There is no right or wrong way to go so long as it works. However, there are a few tricks to consider.

1. Let your subject guide the interviews.

My feeling has always been that most interview subjects are unable to relate their lives in detail from beginning to end. Only once, when working with Henry Hawksworth on his as-told-to autobiography *The Five of Me*, did I have a subject who was able to relate birth to present day in detail in chronological order as we worked. But Hawksworth had just finished several years of intensive psychiatric therapy for multiple personality disorder. He had had to review his life in great detail during the therapy. Everything was fresh for him and he had no problems. In every other case, and in the cases of all the individuals interviewed who have written either authorized biographies or as-told-to autobiographies, the subject would jump from subject to subject, sometimes returning to something discussed earlier to fill in details, sometimes racing ahead because he or she had remembered something the person did not wish to forget. Ultimately you will assemble your notes, tape transcripts, etc., in a logical order based upon the structure you choose to use. To try to force the person to go from period to period will generally result in your subject's not remembering so many details as you will gain by letting the subject handle the pacing.

By contrast, Ken Turan feels that the interview should be handled in the same manner as the book will be written. As he explains: "I do the interviews chronologically as much as possible. If someone thinks of something and starts talking about it, I don't say, 'hold that until next Thursday.' Part of the work of dealing with the transcript is putting it in its right place. I never get in the way of the flow of people's thoughts if I can help it. But it's just much easier for me to deal with it chronologically. The book will be done chronologically. It's much easier when the transcript's done chronologically. And I think it's easier.

"I mean, this process can seem formless to the person you're working with and it's easier to give it that form. Then they can tell they're making progress and they can tell where they are."

Remember that no matter how you do it, you have time. You can always come back to any period, any story, and ask additional questions.

2. Do not start with sensitive personal material.

There are issues about which individuals feel emotionally vulnerable. Divorce, the loss of a loved one, going to jail, bankruptcy, a child in trouble, and various other areas may be perceived as experiences not to be shared with a stranger. These should be covered later in your relationship unless your subject brings them up. Thus if your subject is going through a divorce, your questions might start with a period before the marriage. Or you might start with their profession. Anything that does not call attention to the problem until the person is willing to fully trust you.

3. Look for general areas that may get the person talking.

What was it like growing up in Kansas during the depression? Why did you decide to go into show business? How did you break into politics? When did you first develop your interest in flying? When did you first begin drawing pictures? What made you decide to become a writer? Why did you choose this seemingly inappropriate part of the country for starting your business? When was the first time you really understood what police work was like? What was the first experience you had that made you feel like a real doctor? I didn't know you were interested in painting. What got you started?

4. Clarify points the first time they are raised.

If your subject uses names, technical terms, cities, etc., whose spelling you do not know, get the correct spelling the first time. Likewise ask for details of whatever subject is being raised that you do not understand. Your skill is in telling the subject's life. You do not need to be knowledgeable regarding their business or other aspects of their careers, hobbies, or similar activities.

During the period when auto magnate John DeLorean was being wooed by a number of different publishing companies interested in publishing his book, one company sent an automotive expert to see him. The writer was an expert on cars and could understand every aspect of DeLorean's business and engineering skills. DeLorean refused to work with him.

John asked me if I knew anything about cars. I told him that I only knew how to put in fuel and work the brake, clutch, and gas pedals. I said that even if I did know more, it wouldn't matter. He was an internationally known expert who had developed a new type of car. I would still have to ask what, for him, would undoubtedly be basic questions when it came to anything mechanical. I said that my skill was in coming to understand him and in telling his story in a way that would sound exactly as he would want it if he had developed the writing skills to do it himself. I got the job and the book was on both the *New York Times* and B Dalton Best Seller Lists. The other writer might have done as well, but DeLorean was more willing to clarify points about his business than to risk the chance that he would have to teach an automotive writer how to understand his life.

5. *Don't come to any conclusions.*

When you first get started, the interview may not result in so thorough a set of answers as you will receive later. You may think you know everything but you will not know for many days just how open the person has been. Someone who professes innocence of a crime may later confess but claim that they were not caught fairly. Someone who speaks of loving someone may later express great rage toward the same person.

In one instance a doctor who told me what a close family he had during our early interviews later began talking about hating his father and blaming his father for the death of his older brother. My first inclination was not to waste time on his happy childhood that he seemed to dismiss as an idyllic romp through the early years of life. Because I decided that I had better know everything, I found my early assumptions totally wrong. He had simply never expressed his rage and pain before we had been working together for a few weeks.

6. *Have no time goals other than meeting your deadline.*

There is no way to know at the start how long it will take to get information. Arnold Friberg kept interrupting the story of his life with his comments on the history of painting, something that generally had no place in the book. A long-time criminal whose book ultimately received major, positive reviews in some of the most important newspapers in the nation kept interrupting his stories to seek reassurance that somebody might be interested. He also went off on boring tangents he insisted upon finishing before he got back to the original point.

Your job will be to work with the person's pace, not make some arbitrary decision about how quickly everything should fall into place. And fortunately, in almost every case, your subject will tend to be more thorough and straightforward after he or she is comfortable with your working relationship.

Planning Each Session

When conducting interviews for feature articles I always suggest that the interviewer make a list of questions that he or she wants to cover. These are taken to the interview, reviewed just before meeting with the subject, then ignored. The interview is initially handled without looking at the list.

The reason for this is simple. If the interviewer stays exactly with the list, there is a tendency to not listen to anything the subject says once the answer to the question is given. For example, suppose the question is, "When did you start your business?"

The subject replies, "December 8, 1946," and the interviewer writes down the date, then looks at the next question ignoring the subject who adds, "I remember it well. It was the day I shot my wife and daughter."

By the time the rest of the comment sinks into the interviewer's brain, the subject is answering question number three or four. And by then it's too late to ask about what the interviewer thinks was heard.

Had the interviewer been truly listening instead of worrying about the next question on the list, a followup would have been, "What do you mean that that was the day you shot your wife and daughter?"

Then the subject might reply something to the effect of, "I was coming home from hunting and, as I started to unload my shotgun, I accidentally hit what proved to be a hair trigger. The gun wasn't pointed at anyone, of course. I'm really safety conscious, but the shell hit the walls, ricocheting, and a few almost spent pellets lightly stung their arms. Right then was when I invented the Safety First Trigger Guard so such accidents would be impossible. I made my first million by the next year and began diversifying into the conglomerate I own today."

It is a good story, perhaps the lead, and it would likely have been overlooked had the interviewer been glued to the list.

After the interview is completed, the interviewer unable to think of any other questions, the list is skimmed and unasked questions remaining are checked with a pen. Then these are asked the same way until everything has been answered and new areas explored.

This approach does not work with biography interviews except when talking with friends, co-workers, and acquaintances of the main subject. But the concept of planning each day's interview is important. The difference is that since you have a broad period of the person's life to cover, your subject may be more comfortable having a choice of areas to discuss.

Always review your work enough to know whether or not all your questions have been answered. Some writers, new to interviewing, do not dig deeply enough or tend to talk as much as their subjects, missing important points. These problems are human and you must be willing to return to the subject again and again to clarify details you may need. Do not hesitate to do this as accuracy and completeness are critical, even if you feel a little embarrassed filling in information you feel you should have obtained the first time.

Interviewing is ultimately learned through the experience of conducting interviews. You will be nervous and you may continue to be nervous for many years. Yet you will find that if you are open, attentive, nonjudgmental, accepting, and willing to listen without criticism or shocked reaction, almost everyone, no matter how important, will answer every question you ask, telling you everything you want to know.

SEVEN

Biographies for Children

T ell the truth.

After talking extensively with children's book writers, editors, and publishers, those three words reflect contemporary thinking concerning the writing of children's books.

Tell the truth.

It is hard to know just when reality became a part of children's book writing. There was a period when biographers maintained the fantasy that someone could be all good or all bad when in a position of leadership. An athlete was pure of mind, body, and spirit, a person who never drank, swore, or had more than a chaste relationship with a woman.

A political leader was either all evil, such as an Adolf Hitler, or all good. George Washington was frequently shown to be deep in prayer despite being only marginally involved with religion. Ben Franklin was a serious statesman, inventor, husband, and father who, though mildly eccentric, thought only of the good of others. Except that he was also a womanizer whose letter explaining how a man should choose a mistress deeply offended the Canadian leadership at the time he sought that country's help for the American revolution. Even some of his personal good works evolved from greed, such as his decision to become a postmaster knowing that, with such power, he could assure the mailing of his *Pennsylvania Gazette* while limiting the distribution ability of rival newspaper owners.

For the writer of biographies for children, and for the editors who publish them, the truth about a subject will be a factor in the decision whether or not to publish a book about the person. But once the decision to publish is made, the book must be factual, even though this may mean touching on points of controversy.

Michelle Poploff, a children's book editor for Dell Publishing Company's Yearling division, explained. "We did Martin Luther King and there were these rumors or whatever, some verified, some not, that he was a womanizer. Is that appropriate for an eight-year-old to know or not?

"We didn't leave it out entirely. I don't remember exactly what we said, but I think we did have a part in there where there was talk that Martin was seeing other women or had a roving eye or something like that."

Poploff explained that when the 1988 elections were taking place, the Yearling books division arranged to have biographies of both candidates, Michael Dukakis and George Bush, prepared for publication the moment the results were known. The writers were paid well for their work, each knowing that there would be no publication if their subject did not succeed. These biographies also presented some problems when it came to controversial issues.

"There were many references to Dukakis and his wife, that she was very frivolous and that he was cheap, that he would walk to work, that he would take the subway, that he wouldn't take the car, all that sort of thing. And again we were saying, 'how much of this is important for kids to know?'

"We did, in the final analysis, keep a good part of this because we thought that this is what built his character. We felt that if there was really something malicious, like if he had had an affair or something like that, we probably wouldn't put that in. But there was a part where—we didn't publish this because he didn't win, but had he won, we would have kept it in—there were parts where it said that his wife would buy clothes and keep them in her parents' house because she didn't want him to know how much she was spending. He was sort of a tightwad kind of person. So we kept that in because it sort of helped make up what the book was about, what the real Michael Dukakis was like, so we did end up keeping it.

"But I think if it had been something like affairs or something really pretty awful, we'd keep it out.

"In the Bush biography that we did, of course, publish, we didn't get into anything on the recent political things about Oliver North and all that sort of thing during his term as vice-president. We figured that that would be too difficult to explain and it would take up too many pages, too much time, for that reading level. We just figured that it was too difficult to get into so we left that out."

Poploff continued, discussing a current book that presented concerns because the details were quite in contrast to the fantasies many people held about him. "We're doing the Walt Disney biography right now, and he had a very, very strict, harsh father who used to beat the kids, hit them, and so forth, and all of that's in there. We haven't taken any of that out.

"We have to remember that our audience is second, third, and fourth graders. And we want to give them as much of the human being behind the great person."

This is not to say that the biographer must dwell on the negative. Often only a sentence is desired, such as "Franklin, although married, was reported to have had affairs with other women." The exact wording will vary with the age group, though by high school age such books must be accurate. This does not mean that much of this information should be quoted, though. I would include a copy of Franklin's letter on choosing a mistress in a book for adults. I would mention it in relation to the strain it put on relations with Canada. Yet I would probably not mention it at all (though I would devote a few words or a sentence to the fact that he womanized) when writing for small children.

Uva Dillon of Dillon Press stresses that her concern as an editor and a publisher is not so much what is written but the age group of the readers for which the material is intended. Certain scandalous aspects of a subject's life may be quite appropriate in the biography if it is being written for an age group that can understand it. There is a vast difference between what a third grader can be told and what a seventh grader can understand, for example. She mentioned a book her company published about a writer who was a lesbian and quite comfortable discussing this fact. The book also let this aspect of her life be known, but the book was for a junior high audience that could grasp the meaning of this fact. A younger audience simply wouldn't know what the term meant.

Another factor is the volume of material on a person's life. "For example, we're just getting ready to do a biography of Winston Churchill," explained Dillon. "This is going to be done in the five-to-seven age group. It goes without saying that thousands of pages have been written about him. We can't do a 125- to 150-page biography and do anything but hit the high spots. And we won't even hit the high spots."

If you are not familiar with current biographies for children, you should check with both children's librarians in schools and public libraries, and with bookstore managers maintaining a large children's section. Ask them about the most popular current books in this field for different age groups. Then read them to get a sense of the style and language for the various ages.

Notice whether or not dialogue is used. Some editors insist that you create scenes with dialogue based on the facts as they are known. Others insist that you add nothing that cannot be documented, preferring to see a dramatic narrative without dialogue. The styles expected from you will vary with the company, the series of books if there is a biography series, and/or the editor's personal taste. But in all cases, a book submitted for a particular age group and to a particular publishing company must not vary in style from the others routinely published by that firm. If yours is radically different, you will most likely be rejected.

Ruth Beechick, an editor for Mott Media, commented, "We don't make any attempt to say that absolutely every line is historical." She said that scenes and dialogue may be created "to flesh out facts, to make the biography storylike."

Excerpt from *My Country 'Tis of Thee — Samuel Francis Smith* by Marguerite E. Fitch (Mott Media; Milford, Michigan; 1987). The excerpt is from the time when young Smith, the poet, Baptist minister, and educator who wrote the song "My Country 'Tis of Thee," discovers that his father has died while at work.

"He edged around a tall stack of barrels. 'Oh!' he gasped breathlessly as he stumbled over something soft. He caught his balance just before he fell. Cautiously he reached down and his fingers caught soft clothing. His father was lying in a heap on the floor.

"Samuel dropped to his knees and threw his arms around his father. 'What happened?' he cried out as he gently shook his father. When he placed his ear to his father's chest there was no heartbeat. 'Don't die!' he screamed.

"Samuel's long legs wobbled when he stood up. He swallowed great gulps of air to fight back the terror. His heart beating madly, he ran out onto the wharf and headed for home. He found his mother standing in the doorway, just as he had left her.

" 'What happened? Where is your father?' Mrs. Smith shrieked as Samuel ran up and threw his arms around her.

" 'Father is lying on the warehouse floor,' Samuel explained. Then crisply he added, 'I'm going to get Dr. Boynton. We must get Father home. Ask some neighbors to help.' "

Obviously the incidents described are true but the dialogue and exact actions were told in created story form, an approach that meets with mixed approval by children's book editors.

By contrast, Uva Dillon said that after accurate research, the most important aspect of writing biographies for children and young adults is to "tell the story in an interesting style." Without such a style, "it simply isn't going to be read. Yet it can't be fictionalized." She wants no created dialogue, though she does seek an anecdotal approach as much as possible.

"The hardest part about writing for this age level [juvenile] is deciding what to leave out," explained Scholastic Books' Eva Moore. "I think that what we have to bear in mind is that this is a first book, maybe, that some child will read about this person. It doesn't have to have everything. But it has to be correct. The art of doing this is putting down correct things without distorting the truth."

Moore mentioned the Reverend Weems' myth relating to George Washington, a myth that many small children are taught. She said that while her authors are not expected to debunk such myths, she does not want to see them repeated in the books.

Style

Ruth Beechick recently edited the Sower Series of biographies for Mott Media, a publisher specializing in the Christian market but whose needs are quite similar to those of young adult editors in general. She said:

"One of the major things I look for with writing for children in basically the middle grades, junior high . . . actually adults enjoy reading these . . . are people who can put everything into a story and don't squeeze in too much history. It's kind of obvious when they start putting in some person [who] starts talking, putting in exact dates, just like it's out of a history book. So when they put into their dialogue unnatural memory of historical facts, then this is not very readable.

"Basically it's like certain authors think they have to drop in every bit of historical research they've done. So they're putting it into unnatural dialogue and they're just squeezing it in here and there. It doesn't really add to the story, and so it isn't making history enjoyable for the kids. They have to realize that a lot of their research in doing biographies is not going to get used. They have to select what adds to the story and makes it readable and flows along, and what makes natural dialogue, and that sort of thing. That's one of the major things I've had to combat with some of the writers.

"Before you start in, what major achievement do you want to write about, then look for ways to make that storylike. One of the ones we did was on the Wright brothers. I thought it was especially well done. First there was a race with a Frenchman to see who was going to be first because whoever was first, apparently, was going to get government money. That was before the days of giant corporations. And so as we are reading through this story, we get to live this race step by step. There's some suspense about who's going to win.

"The same kind of thread of a story goes with their trying to solve their scientific problems. You don't know the answer before you start, at least you're not told in this book. You don't know the story of the people and so you get to live it as they're puzzling it out.

"Some writers have become quite skilled at doing this sort of thing, and it seems to me to be one of the major things in doing a biography for children is to make it as storylike as possible."

Eva Moore of Scholastic Books insists that the biographies be in story form. This often means the creation of dialogue as part of the writing. "For younger kids I think it's important to make the story as real as possible. Sometimes that means you have to make up some bits of dialogues. Not pages and pages of it, but to create a scene, for example. You know, for example, in the King book [the biography of Dr. Martin Luther King, Jr.] he tells the story of when he was a little boy, how the white neighbor suddenly decided he couldn't play with his son. And he went home to his mother and she told him that story of prejudice.

"There's no way of knowing what she said exactly, or what he said. But you can kind of make up something that sounds logical, that a child could understand. And then later on, we've drawn from what he's written down. Not only what he said, but what he's written down in his papers or whatever."

Language is no longer restricted except when writing for specialized education programs. There was a time when an author was expected to follow a strict word list. This is no longer the case, in part because children's language skills are generally greater than in the past. Television, while creating some learning problems, has helped with a child's verbalization. The typical child today has a greater vocabulary understanding than children a generation or two earlier.

Choosing the Subject

Michelle Poploff explains that her company did research concerning the types of biographies young children would be interested in reading. The research centered on the way in which historical figures were discussed in the various grades of school. "In second grade you do the explorers or third grade American history or whatever it might be. And then we decided to do some modern-day characters—blacks, whites, minorities, men, women, and just sort of mix it up.

"We do have to try and get figures that are known. Since we are trying to get that school and library market, we do want to fit those people who are going to be taught in the schools and will be kept by the libraries. We do go for high visibility."

The choice is based on someone who is either known or who the children will want to know about. "For example, we're going to do Shirley Temple Black because she also fulfills two qualifications. She is a woman and she was a child star. She was also an ambassador to Ghana, so she's had many different kinds of roles. And of course we've done inventors, and Franklin, Washington, presidents, Indian figures."

"We try not to do sports heroes and entertainers," said Uva Dillon. "We try to do somebody with more substance. Though we do throw in a few of the others, too."

Dillon mentioned that among the subjects for older readers have been feminist writer/lecturer Gloria Steinem, physicist Robert Oppenheimer, and Supreme Court Justice Sandra Day O'Connor. "We really look for someone who's made somewhat of a contribution."

Eva Moore, an editor for the juvenile books line published by Scholastic Books, said that with the younger readers, the selection can be difficult ". . . because the kids don't have any history. We know that there are certain subjects they get in school. Lincoln and Washington they get in school. Anything they might get in school, we try to cover that. Or even if they might hear of anybody. It's hard because you run out of subjects after a while.

"We have several books about Lincoln and several books about Washington. We have like a straight biography of Abraham Lincoln, a regular chronological biography, and then we have a book called *If You Grew Up with Abraham Lincoln.* We have this whole series of 'If You Lived' or 'If You Grew Up' that answers questions about his time and also gives information about him.

"We also have a book called *True Stories about Abraham Lincoln* that is just incidents, little short stories, that cover things that happened to him. That's three I can think of. And now we're working on a series for even younger kids that's picture books.

"We try to think of stories with action, like we're going to try Jacques Cousteau. This is a person who they've heard about, probably on TV, and whose life is filled with action rather than more intellectual."

Moore is hesitant about individuals who are living, famous, but with short careers behind them. Sports figures can get injured and have their careers ended overnight. Both young sports and entertainment figures may find themselves in some type of trouble that makes them undesirable as a book subject. "Unless they have some real history in the sport, and are really, really entrenched. . . . I think we did Hank Aaron when he was vying for the record, and it was done in such a way that we actually did a combination Babe Ruth/Hank Aaron bio."

The exception is with a collective biography. For example, Moore might consider a collection of twenty-four biographies of twenty-four baseball players, or something along those lines. However, she stresses that such books are published with limited enthusiasm because it is not possible to provide much information. Four related biographies collected in one book allow for more effective writing and more interesting reading.

Then, laughing, she added that when it comes to contemporary athletes, "Some of these people you don't really want to know. And you certainly don't want kids to know too much about them. But there are some who really have inspiring stories, and if you can get them out in time, it can do well."

The Christian market has a few more problems than the secular one when choosing a subject. In the past, many subjects were acceptable because of their place in history, even though they were more likely candidates for secular writing. Many of the heroes of the Revolutionary War were men who were radical in their day, including in their attitude toward religious beliefs. Yet there was a time when positive religious qualities were attributed to them even though their lives did not reflect such beliefs. "In my own opinion, Christian publishers have glossed over maybe more of that sort of thing than they should," said Ruth Beechick, "giving people an unrealistic view of those lives.

"The writers working with me . . . we have discussed that when there is a serious problem like that, it has to be touched on and treated as a problem, but then you don't dwell on it. You don't dwell on the womanizing, for instance.

"We had a recent book on Noah Webster where it does come through that he was irascible and hard to get along with and had a temper, and maybe was quite arrogant, also. This was kind of just dropped in along the way, a little hint on it here and there. So you realized that he was like that, but maybe it was glossed over more than it should be."

Beechick explained that the negative aspects need to be mentioned, but not dwelled upon. She stressed that if the negative was too big a part of the life, the Christian publisher would probably not produce the book. "That is, if we knew that ahead of time. Sometimes we don't know until the writer or somebody starts to research."

She continued, saying that when the author, attempting to sell a book to the religious market, is "really scrounging around for proof that he is a Christian, then that really says something in itself. So with a lot of these early Americans, there is that problem where they would make these public statements that sound sort of biblical and God-believing, but they're just deists and not, let's say, satisfying to today's evangelical Christian. So I think that a lot of those people have been treated as Christians in biographies, and I'm sure some have been in our Sower series, that may not even be Christians. I don't think that the Christian publishers today want to carry on a fiction like this.

"Some may be carrying on because the past books were done that way. And there are various reasons why kids aren't exactly getting a true picture these days. But I don't think that Christian publishers deliberately want to do this. I think the picture of their wanting to be honest, at least, is improving year by year with all the Christian publishers. And the writers are just getting better and better all the time."

Research

The attitude authors have toward researching for children's books will vary with the individual. Most advances are much lower than for adult books, requiring the use of resources that do not require extensive travel. There are some as-told-to autobiographies in the young adult (older junior high and high school age groups) but these remain relatively rare. Most authors rely upon other books, magazine and newspaper files, and, occasionally, special collections of letters and other documents. Projects that require extensive travel are generally not considered cost effective by the publisher or the writers.

"I think they go through clippings and articles and any other sources they can get," said Michelle Poploff, referring to the writers with whom she works. "I notice from the Bush and Dukakis books that that was how they did it. Nobody would give them interviews anyway in those particular cases, unless somebody has a contact somewhere.

"And then the book is vetted by an expert in the field. For instance, the Sacajawea book we just did was sent to a professor . . . a know-it-all on American Indians, a Sacajawea expert, and he gave it a quote. Each book of the series has a quote on the back cover by the expert.

"If I'm reading things on Sacajawea, I'm not going to know if they crossed this river or that. I'm taking it that they did their research and that's it. So every manuscript is checked and they're as accurate as possible."

In general, Poploff said that the writer is not expected to go halfway across the country to find diaries or whatever might be in special collections. "Although in some cases, like the Louisa May Alcott who was, of course, a writer, there are excerpts from her letters in her particular biography. I don't know where they got them from. They may be very easy to get.

"We feel comfortable knowing they are vetted at least. We feel that we did the best job possible."

Uva Dillon would like to see as much research for a children's book as is done for an adult biography. "I'm giving you the ideal," she said. "Sometimes you have to settle for a little less, but that is the goal."

Dillon likes to publish books on contemporary individuals such as Jane Goodall and Judy Blume. For these, the company does expect the writer to try to enlist the subject's involvement if possible. Usually this means the granting of one or more interviews when the subject agrees. Judy Blume was one who agreed, for example. "Ideally you try for interviews because you have to do an anecdotal approach, which is really ideal for this age group (third grade). You really have to have firsthand information. Even when a lot has been written about these people, it generally doesn't start early enough and you never know if the information is accurate."

Dillon is quite concerned about conflicting information available to the public. That is another reason why she prefers that biographers of contemporary, living subjects conduct personal interviews whenever possible.

Although some of the juvenile books for Scholastic are concerned with living people, most of the research is done through sources other than interviews, Eva Moore explained. However, the manuscript for a book about a living or recently deceased individual is sent to experts connected with the person. Also, the author is expected to use as much firsthand material—diaries, articles, and other items written by the subject—as can be obtained. This is supplemented by secondary sources.

The children's market, whether for the religious publishers or the general trade, has changed radically in recent years. It has become a smaller version of the adult market and must be respected accordingly. Thorough research, accurate anecdotes, and a lack of forced education are all critical for this market.

EIGHT

How Can You Say That About Them?

J im Bacon, a long-time Hollywood columnist and reporter for the Associated Press, discussed the reasons presidential biographies had changed in recent years. He mentioned that before John Kennedy, a president's personal life was considered off-limits for reporters. They knew what was taking place. They just chose not to tell the public.

Kennedy was the last president to have such an arrangement with the press, a fact that kept Kennedy's womanizing a rumor instead of a part of contemporary awareness. "Marilyn [Monroe] used to tell me about her relationship with Jack Kennedy all the time," Bacon explained, delighting in the stories she would relate. But he never repeated the information while the president was alive. "It was only when Nixon began doing to the country what Kennedy had done in private that we began writing about it," Bacon explained.

The problem with writing contemporary and historical biographies and as-told-to autobiographies is that the facts seldom reflect our fantasies. We frequently undertake a project because we see great good or great bad in an individual. What we are uncomfortable discovering are the gray areas, the dirty little secrets that are frequently a part of almost everyone's past.

Most of us never think about the moral and ethical issues behind what we write until we encounter the problem. For example, when I acted as coauthor for car manufacturer John DeLorean, I was telling the story of a man who had gained international headlines as a result of his arrest for cocaine trafficking. The press reports indicated that he had gotten himself involved in a drug deal in order to finance DeLorean Motor Cars, a company that was running out of money.

My circumstances were unusual in working with John. I was on a work-for-hire arrangement with the publisher, a company specializing in religious books and books that appeal to both the religious and secular markets. Work-for-hire involves a flat fee rather than royalties, the author not sharing in the copyright or subrights income. The editor was uncomfortable with DeLorean, uncertain whether or not he was ready to tell the truth about his case. I was asked to independently cross-check everything that was said so that nothing went in the book that was not accurate. To my horror, he was telling the truth and I found that he had been set up by an FBI agent who admitted to changing evidence, a Drug Enforcement Administration (DEA) agent who admitted to lying to both the grand jury and the trial jury, another DEA agent who was so ashamed of his actions that he quit his position and testified for the defense, and others. DeLorean had agreed to cooperate only after he was informed that his daughter would be murdered if he didn't. A government informant, allegedly with the awareness of one or more agents, said on the telephone, in front of at least one trustworthy witness, that the child's head would be placed in a shopping bag and given to John if he did not go along with the scheme. The day before he flew to California where the arrest occurred, DeLorean wrote a letter telling all and revealing that he believed he was going to be killed by people he assumed to be part of the Mafia after he arrived.

The arrest was the culmination of more than three months of hell in which DeLorean desperately tried to raise money through legitimate sources. Having been in line for chairman of General Motors when he resigned from that company to start his own, De-Lorean had important contacts throughout the world. He spent those three months visiting one hundred cities, making thirty or more telephone calls a day, and trying to sleep only four hours a night, the minimum rest he felt his body needed. Naturally he was always exhausted, so he drank several pots of coffee to awaken each morning, took Seconal sleeping pills at night, and in between used large quantities of wine with dinner to relax. He also arranged to have a Canadian over-the-counter product, illegal in the United States, brought to him for his headaches. The compound contained half aspirin, half codeine, a highly addictive narcotic. He also smoked marijuana regularly, obtaining it from friends and trying to use it to relax.

Suddenly I was faced with an ethical problem. If I told the literal truth about DeLorean's actions during the period just before his arrest, some people would be sympathetic. They would see a man who was desperate, exhausted, willing to do anything to save the jobs of his workers and the future profits of his company. They would recognize that his judgment was impaired, his actions borne of desperation.

Others, naive in the ways of the illegal drug world, would say that if DeLorean was using marijuana, he must also be dealing in cocaine. The fact that the two drugs are radically different and that in the world in which DeLorean moved, the sources were quite separate, would not be understood. Although I had statements concerning DeLorean's innocence both from direct interviews with some of the law enforcement officials and from testimony under oath in court, I feared mentioning the marijuana. In reality, the regular use of the codeine/aspirin combination was far more dangerous, codeine being a highly addicting substance sold under controlled conditions in the United States. But the readers might not understand all this. I was afraid that mentioning the marijuana use in the book would result in an unfair backlash against him.

Ultimately I decided to withhold the story about the marijuana. I listed everything else with which he was involved, including the codeine/aspirin combination. But I omitted the fact that he also smoked "pot."

Why am I telling it now? Because this type of ethical consideration is one you may face yourself.

When Douglas Ginsberg was under consideration for the Supreme Court, he admitted that as a typical child of the 1960s, he had smoked marijuana. It was one of the reasons he was denied a position on the bench. Yet as several journalists commented, smoking marijuana in the 1960s was a rite of passage for many young men and women. They have gone on to be responsible citizens, government and business leaders, who have families and consider their past actions to be wrong. Thus any biography of someone raised in that era may find the use of one or more recreational drugs was a part of their background.

Likewise, the prohibition era was a time when many youths delighted in obtaining bootleg whiskey. Lawyers, judges, doctors, and others all had their sources for safe homemade alcohol that was illegal to possess or consume.

Sex can be even more of a problem, especially if you look upon a historic figure as heroic for their public accomplishments and have not previously thought about their private life. For example, we are taught in school to idealize our nation's founding fathers as though they were above reproach. This may be fine for the school books and for those who like to remember someone in much the same manner as Parson Weems, the story-telling pseudobiographer. But it is not fine for the objective author.

Think about the top leaders of our nation during the period of the American Revolution. The only reason we glorify them is because they won the war and many of their ideas form the backbone of our nation. If we were alive at the time they were agitating against the British, most of us would have been disgusted with them.

The truth is that most of the founding fathers were political agitators who did not respect existing authority. They rebelled against a tradition of government that went back centuries in England. Many of them were descendants of people who had been criminals before coming to the colonies and their values were not respected.

Even the religious field is fraught with minefields. For example, Kathryn Kuhlman was one of the most famous faith healers in the United States during the period ranging from the 1950s through her death on February 20, 1976. Millions believed in her abilities and she was the subject of both love and controversy. When she died, both publishers and writers recognized that her life story had an instant audience of millions and several books were commissioned.

It would seem that the image of Kathryn Kuhlman could not be a moral or ethical concern for biographers. Here was a woman who had dedicated her life to the ministry. She was born in 1907 and began preaching the Bible while a teenager. She lived in poverty. She lived in wealth. But she was always available to others, her dedication to the ministry never questioned, even by her enemies. Thus the biographies should have been simple, straightforward, and easy to write. Except for the truth.

Perhaps the greatest secret in Kathryn Kuhlman's life was the six-year period she spent as the wife of Burroughs A. Waltrip. Periodically the story was told in the press, once in the early 1950s by the *Akron Beacon Journal*, a newspaper in Akron, Ohio. Another time it was revealed in 1970 by syndicated columnist Lester Kinsolving. Yet the publicity was limited and Kathryn was so embarrassed by it that she usually denied it had taken place.

The facts were quite simple. Waltrip, an evangelical minister, was a married man with children who traveled as a preacher. In 1937 he visited the Denver, Colorado, Revival Tabernacle, preaching for two months. Kuhlman, eight years younger than Waltrip, was also there, working full time. She was enamored with his looks and his style, inviting him back in the fall of that year. He apparently had been impressed with her as well because he returned with his wife and two sons—the wife, Jessie, seemingly jealous of Kuhlman's good looks and intelligence.

No one is certain exactly when the affair began. All that is known is that Jessie and the boys returned to Austin, Texas, where the boys had to enroll in school during Waltrip's second visit to Denver. However, he lied to the parishioners and claimed that his wife had deserted him. He claimed to have begged her to return, something he said she refused to do. Then, reluctantly, according to his statements, he had to move on without her. He traveled to Mason City, Iowa, establishing a popular public and radio ministry.

Kathryn Kuhlman joined Waltrip in Mason City, having an affair that they made public after his divorce was final, and they announced that they would be married.

For six years the couple tried working and living together. Neither believed in adultery or divorce despite the fact that they had committed both. Between their sense of guilt and the hostility of those who were aware of what had taken place, both their ministries went into a decline. Eventually Kuhlman could take no more, leaving her husband, a man she adored until her death, divorcing him and continuing on her own.

The problem was that many people, including biographers, were not ready to cope with the idea that Kathryn Kuhlman could be anything but a saint. Most made the decision to gloss over the incident, usually saying that if she did not discuss it, neither should they. Only Jamie Buckingham chose to tackle the issue openly, feeling that Kuhlman would have wanted the truth known. No embarrassing little secrets were spared in the book *Daughter of Destiny*, a book that became a best seller in the religious market, something most of the "nicer" biographies failed to achieve. And Kuhlman came across as a full human being, a complex individual whose efforts seemed all the greater considering the pain she had experienced as a result of her decisions.

The reverse problem is facing contemporary religious biographers of television evangelists. If a man has been found to have sex with prostitutes, misuse contributions, and otherwise act in a reprehensible manner, how do you handle the good you find he has done? The pure villain is easier to write. The whole person, who may have good mingled with the bad, is less comfortable.

There are also times when people change, their pasts radically different from their present. This is especially true with individuals in politics where myth is often the reality for the average person.

Neil Baldwin, when writing the William Carlos Williams book, discovered that his subject was a self-proclaimed womanizer. "I had access to love letters written to him by various lovers his wife didn't even know about, which I was reading, then sealing in envelopes until the year 2020 or whatever [in accordance with Williams' wishes]. But I had to read them first.

"I had access to information of that type and it came down to writing the book and I could have repressed it. I couldn't deal with the extent of his promiscuity, which is still not really fully known. But you know, his wife was no longer living. His sons knew about it. He confessed to his wife before he died. I just thought it was overwhelming, either real or imagined.

"So my editor was reading the manuscript and she called me up and said, 'What happened to all the women?'

"I said, 'What do you mean?'

"She said, 'None of them are mentioned in there.' I had totally self-suppressed it without even being aware of it. I had placed a moral standard on him that was really not correct at that level.

"I guess I just couldn't face it.

"She said, 'You've got to put it back in. You left it all out.'

"I did. That was that. Nobody complained. I did it in very nice little poetic ways. It was a real lesson to me. It was a lesson to the biographers, a sort of code of ethics. It was a lesson in the standards that you hold. If you had no filtering system, then you'd have something that's twenty-five thousand pages long, so you're obviously making discriminations. But you can't make a value judgment on the facts. You can arrange the facts in such a way that they combine to make an impression that you want to create.

"I don't speculate. There is not one 'probably,' or 'could have,' or 'might have' in the book. I had to have reasonable certainty of something corroborated, like, three different ways or I didn't put it in. I hate biographies that say 'so and so' may well have been or 'so and so' may well have done. That's not the way to go about it.

"I learned a lot from that first biography concerning what you can discriminate against and what you can't. That's the first test of a really good biographer. I also don't think people realize how many judgment calls you have to make. On that one page there might be twenty-five different decisions to make about a fact. But like I say, a value judgment is quite different from 'well, it seems like so and so went to a party and . . .' But like he had three affairs in one month. I'm not going to judge that. It's not appropriate."

Another approach to the problem arose for me when I worked on the Peter Lawford biography. The more I studied his notes, the more uncomfortable I became. Peter was a child abuse victim, raised as a girl by his emotionally disturbed mother, then subject to sexual abuse by his nanny and her best friend when he was ten. He came to Hollywood at the end of the studio glamour era when the studio executives controlled the lives and public images of the stars. They also abused the stars, especially the younger ones, frequently using drugs to keep children working all day and sleeping quietly at night. The executives were responsible for everything from many of the emotional and drug problems of former child stars like Judy Garland to creating romances that were photographed for the fan magazines.

One of the discoveries I made concerned a friend of Peter's, a woman known as a good-time girl who was determined to be a star in the pictures. Numerous friends and co-workers, many of whom did not know each other, told substantially the same stories, unknowingly corroborating one another's statements. By the time the interviews were complete, the facts were as Peter had stated them in his notes and they were not pleasant ones. That starlet's name was Nancy Davis and there would have been no moral dilemma in writing about her had she not married an actor named Ronald Reagan, ultimately becoming first lady of the United States.

There were stories of Reagan as well. He was less ambitious than Nancy Davis, yet more created by the studios. He was an Air Force Captain in World War II who never left California. He became airsick the only time he flew, and that trip was approximately twenty miles to Catalina Island. His role was to make movies at the Hal Roach Studios, a studio converted for training and propaganda films, primarily, and dubbed "Ft. Wacky" by those who knew about its use.

Reagan was married to Jane Wyman at the time, a marriage arranged and encouraged by the studios on January 25, 1940. (She would later be quoted as saying that going to bed with Reagan was like sleeping with your brother.) They were both interviewed concerning the problems of separation, anxiety, and loneliness during the war, though the truth was that they lived together the entire time, Reagan commuting home every night.

There would have been no concerns about telling the stories of Nancy Davis, Ronald Reagan, and Peter Lawford during this period if Reagan had not become president of the United States. Unfortunately we have a tendency to hold the president and his wife above reproach. No matter what someone has been like in the past, once they become president, we assume that he is meeting the highest standards of honesty, integrity, and intelligence.

The question I faced was how to handle an extremely disreputable history. Did I forget the stories of Peter, Robert Walker, and Nancy Davis driving back and forth to Phoenix, Arizona, so she could visit her parents? The trips involved activities that many people would find offensive given her present position. Did I ignore the affairs that were not only an integral part of his life but also reflected the morality of the times and the attitudes within the studios?

My questions were decided for me because of both the need to be accurate concerning the period of history and facts that were uncovered during the Reagans' time in power. First, many of Reagan's war stories were not history, they were scenes from movies in which he had either had a part or witnessed firsthand. The fantasy role he had played in helping with the propaganda effort of World War II had become real life in his mind, something to be used when making decisions about contemporary problems.

Second, there was the growing awareness that Nancy Reagan was a fraud. She "wrote" a book on grandparents, one of her special projects as first lady. The fact that the book was ghosted came as no surprise to anyone. The fact that Mrs. Reagan had not bothered to meet most of the subjects of the book was of greater concern. Then it was learned that she and the president had not even bothered to meet his son's first child, their grandson, despite the boy's birth more than a year earlier.

The more I looked into what was happening in the White House, the more I realized that the period about which I was writing had had an impact on decisions being made forty years later. Some of the stories were not nice. Some were humorous. All seemed to have importance for anyone trying to understand the present era. I made the decision to go with them, accepting the criticism I would receive, knowing that they might otherwise be lost to history.

The biography of Peter Lawford sold extremely well, some of the stories, taken out of context, having been picked up by a variety of magazines. Some of the readers were irate, referring to the stories as rude, crude, and obscene (Patricia and I were called "world class gossips" by one reviewer). Some of the readers accepted them in context, not really caring one way or another. And some, including both other biographers and editors, felt that what had been said might prove to be a contribution to historic understanding.

There are other extremes of concern, though. While doing the same Lawford book, I learned that there were photos Peter took that showed President Kennedy cavorting with Marilyn Monroe in the bathtub. They would undoubtedly have commanded a large sum of money in the tabloid press and might have increased the sale of the book if they had been used. However, there was no purpose to such images other than pandering to prurient curiosity. Thus the Reagans went in, the pictures stayed out, and again the decision was an ethical one that required responding to the specific circumstances.

Even this book raises a moral dilemma. While talking about "high moral standards," I am revealing stories, not all of which have been published before. Thus the chapter becomes titillating, in theory a selling point for a volume on writing. Yet unless these issues are raised for writers, unless the examples are understood when you first begin researching this type of book, you are headed for trouble. It is often easier to discover the stories that make people laugh, cringe, or say, "How can he say that about them?" than you might realize. Thus I am risking being criticized for violating the same moral issues that I am raising, a situation that raises the exact same concerns that all of us face when writing biographies and, frequently, as-told-to autobiographies.

Perhaps these sound extreme. However, the truth is that all lives have their "dirty little secrets." One of the most liberal of the U.S. Supreme Court Justices of the last fifty years had been a member of the Ku Klux Klan in his youth. Richard Nixon, so corrupt he was forced to resign from office, was also the man who restored relations with China, perhaps opening that country to the ideas that ultimately led to the student democratic uprising of 1989. Charles Lindbergh, the pioneer aviation hero, was a supporter of Hitler's Nazi movement before World War II.

There is good and bad with everyone and, as a biographer, you cannot gloss over this reality. How far you go, how much you reveal, will depend upon the nature of the book, the intended audience, and similar factors. Yet we are no longer writing during a period when these issues can be ignored. Both the editors and the public want truth, not the myths of a Parson Weems, yet the truth is not necessarily what we truly want to read.

Carl Rollyson, the author of books on Marilyn Monroe, Lillian Hellman, and others, ran into a different type of ethical problem while working on his biography of Martha Gellhorn. Gellhorn was still living when he began the book that would detail the life of a brilliant writer who also was one of Ernest Hemingway's wives. Although many of her actions throughout life would not be considered shocking today, they were not something talked about in "polite society" at the time. The results are "dirty little secrets" that Rollyson encoutered and that, if he quotes them, will bring about her ire. As he explained:

"There's a kind of funny, amusing story to be told about her first 'marriage' that I would put in quotation marks, so to speak, because she wasn't actually married. She spent some years in the late twenties and early thirties in France and started living with a marquis, Bertrand de Juvenal, who was from a prominent French family. And they lived together for a while.

"Her St. Louis family was scandalized and his father was a diplomat who was somewhat embarrassed. They kind of concocted this story to the press about being married. And they had some sort of ceremony with a priest, but it wasn't really legalized. And yet this appeared in a big announcement thing in the St. Louis papers about her being a Baroness. And the curious thing is that up until and including the marriage to Hemingway, through the mid-forties, in most standard reference accounts this other, so-called marriage was referred to as a marriage and his being her second husband. Then after the war, after her divorce, then suddenly this disappears.

"If you look at most reference books published after, say, 1948, if they mention Juvenal at all, they might mention him as a kind of liaison or traveling companion, something like that. The whole relationship suddenly becomes very cloudy.

"In a way that's rather important in my book in the sense that that happens at a time when she's very much modeling her career and styling herself. I think there are a lot of revealing things to be said about her in just telling that story about what happened.

"As recently as a couple of years ago, she told a woman who was doing a book on war correspondents that, oh, this was just a silly misunderstanding of the press, that she and Juvenal had checked into a hotel or something on a registration card, and had to say they were married or something. And some reporter saw this, and this was how it happened. That's not anywhere near the truth. Nowhere near the truth . . .

"I've interviewed some of her childhood friends who remember vividly that whole period of her life." But Gellhorn refused to be interviewed for the book, expressing her displeasure by not agreeing to cooperate.

"Gellhorn, actually, has been actively hostile to my book. She told people not to talk to me and she's even been, not directly but through a representative of hers, sent threatening letters to my publisher." She told the publisher that Rollyson will not be permitted to quote from any of her works. She also claimed to have absolute right over her person and image. "I can't even put a photograph of her in my book. The claims are rather outrageous." Gellhorn has made herself a public figure, and Rollyson is well within his rights to produce the book.

Rollyson mentioned a note he had received from Gellhorn. "I hate all biographies. I hope there's never one done of me."

"I mean, she's eighty years old and she said, 'I can't afford to die because I know someone will write of my life and it will be detestable.'" Oddly a letter was sent to Rollyson's publisher claiming that an authorized biographer had been assigned by Gellhorn so there was no reason for the publisher to deal with someone like Rollyson.

"So when I get that kind of response, she hasn't exactly been level with me. I'm not out to get her. It's not a book to get her. But I feel a little tough-minded about such things. I feel that I pick people who are public figures and then, at a certain point in their lives, they suddenly turn into control freaks. And frankly, I'm not out to consciously hurt or damage anybody, but they have a kind of place in history already, and what they try to do, what I think [Lillian] Hellman tried to do, was to control that. And yet if they were on the other end, and many of them have been reporters and journalists and so on, I think in someone else they would find that behavior detestable."

Rollyson also discussed a story he did withhold. This one related to his biography of actress Marilyn Monroe. While researching that book, he discovered that there was someone who had helped her obtain drugs during her early years of substance abuse. The man was not a criminal. He was a close friend who truly cared about her, wanting to ease some of the pain in her personal life, give her pleasure, and gain her favor. He had no idea that she would become an addict to such a degree that the drugs would destroy her life. He helped her through loving kindess and, only in hindsight, did he realize the problems he may have caused her. Although the story was important in the sense that it added a piece to the puzzle that was Monroe in her early years, Rollyson felt that it would cause the man needless anguish and shame. He had mixed feelings about what he should do, ultimately deciding to omit it from his book.

Ethical Concerns

Imagine that you are writing someone else's book, either as a ghost or with credit to be given on the cover. Now imagine that the individual wants to lie. "It's my story," the subject may say. "You've got no concerns. Just tell it the way I tell you. That's what you're being paid to do."

Such comments are routinely heard by everyone who becomes involved with such a project. But what is right in such a case? What are the morals and ethics involved?

The Issue of Libel

Before any other considerations, there is the libel issue. The First Amendment to the Constitution of the United States reads: "Congress shall make no law respecting an establishment of religion, or prohibiting the free exercise thereof; or abridging the freedom of speech, or of the press; or of the right of the people peaceably to assemble, and to petition the government for a redress of grievances."

What does this mean for you as a writer? You can publish anything you desire. You do not have to be accurate. You do not have to have someone's permission to publish. Your writing may use foul language and crude images. You may produce racist material, sexist material, text that is degrading to almost everyone. At least as early as Ben Franklin's *Pennsylvania Gazette* there were stories about sexual assignations within the community. And even today there are newspapers that delight in gossip and scandal.

You can publish pornography. You can publish your own version of the Bible. Nothing is taboo.

Until after it is in print.

Although the Constitution allows us to print lies, various state laws say that there may be penalties to pay if we fail to tell the truth, especially about another person. This is where the libel laws come into play because libel, in its simplest form, is telling one or more falsehoods about another person.

Yet libel is the most serious of the offenses a writer can commit in the eyes of the court. With libel there is often no relief from the penalties imposed. You can create a corporation and use it as a shield against many types of lawsuit penalties. In most instances the corporation is liable for debts equal to the assets of the corporation, present and future, but the men and women who have formed that corporation are not personally liable. With libel, the liability is with the person who has not told the truth. Dissolving the corporation or declaring corporate bankruptcy does not absolve you of the debt. Even personal bankruptcy does not save you from ultimately having to pay a libel suit judgment in many cases.

In theory libel is a very simple matter. You tell the truth and you are protected against losing a libel suit. You make false statements and you may pay a penalty. But there is actually more to it than that. Sometimes the situation depends upon your subject. At other times it depends upon how you document your case.

Let us explore three very real issues, all taken from writing concerns encountered by authors working on biographies. Notice the issues that have to be raised if you are going to protect yourself from losing in a court of law.

(Note: Anyone can sue anyone else for just about everything, providing the person can find a lawyer willing to bring such a lawsuit. It is not the writer's job to protect the publisher from being sued because of your book. If it was, almost none of us would be writing because such protection is literally impossible. Instead, it is the writer's job to protect the publisher from losing a libel suit and this is something you can learn to do, as you shall see.)

First, a few definitions to show the problem as the courts have defined it. When you say something that defames or injures someone's name or reputation, you are said to have slandered that person. When you do the same thing in writing, including doing it in the form of a script that is read over radio and television, the defamation or injury is called libel.

Every state has established case law concerning libel. However, most writers follow the first U.S. Supreme Court ruling on the matter, a case called *New York Times v. Sullivan* that was heard in 1964. This law concerned the rights of a public official acting in a public capacity. It said that the public official must prove that there was actual malice based upon the publisher and/or writer's knowledge that the material was false. A second part of the ruling held that even when there was no provable malice, the writer and/or publisher had the obligation to check to see if the material was accurate. If not, it was libelous because of "reckless disregard" or whether or not it was false.

The results of the decision were quite simple and easy for any of us to follow. To commit libel against a public figure, you first must defame the individual as described earlier. This basically means that you must lie.

Then this defamation or lie must be obviously against the person suing. This means that if I write the statement: "Most U.S. senators are corrupt and steal from their constituents," Senator Horatio P. Fogbreath cannot sue me for libel based solely on that statement. He was not specifically named, nor was his reputation sullied. On the other hand, if Senator Fogbreath is the senator from New York and I make the statement that all current New York senators are corrupt and steal from their constituents, he would begin to have a case against me because there are only two such individuals and my comment is directed toward both of them. Most important of all, I can hide the reference through the use of a nickname or similar device, but the identification remains if it is obvious to the reader about whom I am speaking.

And finally, the statement must be published. Until such time as it appears in print and is made available for someone else to read, it is not libel. Thus writing a letter with deliberately defamatory statements is not libelous until the letter is passed on to someone else, either through mailing or some other way.

Libel Defense

There are three defenses against libel. The most important is truth, a situation that does not relate to accuracy. If you say an action took place, you must be able to prove that it did. The fact that you are accurately quoting the words of someone who "should know" does not make it factual. It is your obligation to cross-check what was said.

In August 1989, twenty-five years after Sullivan, the case of *David Price v. Viking Penguin, Inc.* resolved, in part, the issue of accuracy and truth. The case related to statements for and against FBI Special Agent David Price who had been assigned to the Pine Ridge Indian Reservation in the South Dakotas during the early 1970s. This was the period when the Wounded Knee occupation occurred, during which time two other FBI agents were shot and killed. Price was an investigator who was discussed in the book *In the Spirit of Crazy Horse*, a book published by Viking Penguin that was essentially sympathetic to the Indian viewpoint. This meant that there were statements made that were derogatory toward the government, including Special Agent Price who felt he had been libeled.

The resolution of the case was an important one. The suit hinged, in part, on whether or not accurate quotes were libelous. Essentially the court held that so long as opinions were expressed and both sides were given roughly equal space to present their opposing views, the fact that one side might be an accurate quote, though libelous, did not make the author guilty of libel. While an accurately quoted libelous statement is still libelous, by also quoting the opposite view and giving it roughly equal weight, the writer eliminated malice and presented a factual account of the moods and attitudes of the people.

This means that truth does not have to be a totally resolved subject. You do not have to have "the answer" for something where truth cannot be determined with certainty because there are too many believable, conflicting statements, such as those concerning what took place on the Pine Ridge Reservation. However, the "truth" is determined by the accurate and relatively equal reporting of both sides without you, the writer, showing a bias toward one side or the other. You commit libel when you accurately report a false statement. You do not commit libel when you accurately report opposing statements, one of which has to be false, though where the truth is unresolved by all parties involved.

Next there is the issue of consent. If a public figure chooses to reveal his or her life to a writer, and if the writer makes an effort to be accurate, the subject generally cannot sue for defamation. This is based on the idea that the subject understood the risk that he or she might be defamed when agreeing to the interview and took the risk.

This issue was modified somewhat when former Green Beret Doctor Jeff MacDonald successfully sued author Joe McGinnis concerning his book *Fatal Vision*. MacDonald agreed to have McGinnis write his biography based upon the belief that McGinnis was sympathetic to MacDonald's allegations that he was innocent of the murders of his wife and daughters for which he had been charged. McGinnis claimed to be his friend and wrote frequent letters sympathetic to MacDonald in order to maintain MacDonald's trust at the same time that McGinnis became convinced that MacDonald was the sole killer. What started as a friendly project ended as a deception that ultimately added public support to the conviction of MacDonald.

There were many issues in the lawsuit that MacDonald ultimately won against the author. These included McGinnis' deliberate lies to maintain the subject's trust, what amounted to a breach of contract based on the original agreement, and even such questions as to how thoroughly McGinnis checked all the facts. By the time the case came to court, investigators such as former FBI Special Agent Ted Gunderson could prove that other suspects were known at the time the book was written and that these suspects were not interviewed.

While the McGinnis suit was not a libel case per se, and while the consent issue remains as primary case law, you must be careful to not use deception when working directly with a subject. Should your attitude change, this must be made clear. And at all times, any information that results in your taking a different approach than agreed upon must be carefully researched. Had McGinnis interviewed everyone locatable who had allegedly been involved with the murder, and had he not made admittedly false statements to MacDonald in order to retain the subject's trust, MacDonald's lawsuit would probably have been unwinnable and quite likely would not have come to court.

Finally, a writer can make a fair comment that may be negative. This is no different from the critic's role when a critic expresses his or her dislike for a play, a concert, or a book. However, fair comment must be made without provable malice. If I tell a publisher that I think that Richard Nixon was the most corrupt president in history and I'm going to write a scathing book telling all, then I have malice toward the former president. I could be sued for libel despite the fact that the president was forced to resign.

By contrast, if I plan an objective book and, by the time I have completely explored all the facts, I come to believe that Nixon was the most corrupt president in history, it would not be libelous to write something to the effect of: "By the time I finished sifting through thousands of documents, listening to hundreds of hours of tape recordings, and interviewing hundreds of people involved with Nixon both personally and professionally, I came to the conclusion that he was the most corrupt president in history." There is no malice in the comment and thus it will be considered fair comment, even though it is negative.

Some writers like to think that they can get away with any statement so long as they print a retraction or correction. Sometimes this is deliberate (malice). Most times it is not. A writer gets careless and rushes a story into print because everything seems all right. Most sources have been checked. Attempts to reach the subject or people who can accurately provide a differing opinion have been unsuccessful, though within a relatively short time frame. And the writer feels that the statement is probably right, the story is a good one, and a deadline must be met. Then, after the article is published, all the facts become known and the writer finds that the statements were false. An immediate retraction is printed and the writer may truly be contrite. Unfortunately this still constitutes malice, the only saving grace being that most courts have reduced the ultimate penalties rewarded under such circumstances.

Some people are exempt from libel suits, but never in all circumstances. For example, it has generally ruled that major public officials — presidents, governors, senators, congressional representatives — cannot be sued for libel for statements made in their official capacity. This usually means a situation such as when the statement is made in Congress during debate over a particular issue. Equally important, a journalist cannot be sued for quoting the exact statement made by that politician, even though the statement is known to be false by all parties involved.

Even here there is an exception. The journalist must not have malicious intent involved with quoting the libelous statement made by the public official acting in an official capacity. And this situation extends even to someone who may have left office in disgrace, such as with the following example.

The Crooked President

Richard Nixon, former president of the United States, was a crook, right? The man resigned from office rather than becoming the nation's first president to be impeached. A real sleaze, right?

Come on, be honest. You think this way. I don't care if you're an ardent Republican die-hard who points with pride to the fact that Nixon was an important international statesman who opened dialogue and trade with mainland China. When it came to the domestic side, this crook would do anything for power. Look at Watergate. Look at the plans he and former Attorney General John Mitchell made to hold antiwar demonstrators in makeshift concentration camps for up to one-and-a-half years if necessary. Look at . . .

Got your attention? Having trouble arguing with me? Even if you're saying that the good far outweighs the bad, that other presidents have been equally bad or worse, they just haven't been caught, you're still leaning toward my opinion. At least a little. I mean, come on, everybody knows the guy was a crook. So what crime did he commit?

Wait a minute. Don't start reciting chapter and verse about Watergate. Remember President Gerald Ford granting Richard Nixon a pardon from prosecution for any crime he may have committed? Richard Nixon has not been convicted of a crime. Richard Nixon is not going to be charged with a crime. Because he is a disgraced public figure, calling him a crook is probably not going to result in a libel suit against you. Public opinion would not be on his side. But technically, Richard Nixon is not a crook and calling him one is a libelous statement.

So how do you get around that problem? It is easy. You tell the truth. You discuss Watergate and the massive cover-up as you can document them from the tape recordings available through the National Archives in Washington, the Watergate proceedings recorded in the Congressional Record, the confessions through books and trial transcripts of his aides, and the other documents that exist. You present all the evidence. Where appropriate, you counterpoint with his published testimony and any statements in the books he has written. You ideally make an effort to conduct an interview with him because, even if you are turned down, you are still showing fairness. You are giving the person a chance to reply to the issues raised by the public record.

When you are done, your reader will probably say, "Why, Richard Nixon was a crook." The reader might say, "Wow, what a brilliant, far-sighted statesman on the international front. I don't know why no one started trying to open mainland China before. But domestically, he sure did some crooked things."

The reader's reaction is fine. The reader is expressing an opinion based on the facts. But neither the opinion nor the objective presentation of information that led to the expressing of that opinion is libelous. Only your saying that Richard Nixon is a crook when the man was never convicted of any crime could be subject to legal action.

The Kidnapped Child

A student of mine has a dramatic story about a woman who went through the nightmare of having her child kidnapped by her ex-husband. She was the custodial parent by court order. He was in the Air Force. He took his son, an act that was kidnapping because he was not the person with legal custody, and then with the help of someone in the Air Force, he managed to flee the area and have his whereabouts kept from his ex-wife.

The student was all excited. The Air Force had helped the husband kidnap the child and secrete the boy somewhere. The Air Force was involved with a cover-up because it took many months for the mother to find her son. The mother even hired a private investigator who reported a cover-up by the Air Force.

My student saw drama in the story, passion, intrigue, and a national scandal. She also had a strong woman's story with an ultimately happy ending. It was a perfect story—perfectly libelous.

As I explained to my student, the basic story of the mother's fight to find her son, along with the ultimate reunion, was definitely a good story to write about. But the background she was relating was probably nonsense. It was highly unlikely that the U.S. Air Force, under direct orders by a member of the Joint Chiefs of Staff, deliberately allowed a kidnapping. It was almost as unlikely that the commander of the air base where the ex-husband was stationed knew what was going on.

To avoid the libel issue, there were several steps that had to be taken. First, she had to learn about the father. Service records are public records. The mother could get her husband's service record through the Freedom of Information Act or, in most cases, by calling the base public information officer who would refer her to the appropriate person, probably in Washington. The release would be a formality.

Then she had to note how the mother had gone after information about her husband and son. Who, exactly, did she contact? What channels did she pursue? And what about the private investigator? How had he gone about his work? With whom had he spoken? If he used special "confidential sources" and won't release a name, this may be nonsense and he may have reached someone who couldn't do anything but didn't want to admit that he could not. Claiming that there was a "cover-up" sounds believable enough under the circumstances, though one statement by a "reliable" or "confidential" source is hardly meaningful.

The next step would be to go to the base commander to discuss the matter. What was known and by whom? What occurred or might have occurred to allow the father to take the child out of the area? Remember that the fact that he did not have legal custody would not be something that would be obvious to anyone else. Under normal circumstances the child would show no fear, would probably have no awareness that anything was wrong. After all, the child was just going with his father. In fact, whatever the situation with the transportation to another state, it may very well have been legal, proper, and aboveboard given what everyone involved might have known. The only area that might have been subject to question concerned whether or not someone was asked to lie about where he had gone. Obviously the base commander might have been involved with a cover-up. Or the base commander might refuse to investigate. It might be necessary to go to the commander-in-chief of the Air Force. But logic in a story like this tells you that it is far simpler than the conspiracy theory and, until it is carefully checked, point by point, there is a chance that the emotional reaction could create a situation where libel is involved.

What Is Truth?

It is easy to talk about facts when discussing libel. But what are facts? Some reporters like to say that if three separate people tell the same story, then it is accurate. They feel they can use it without losing a libel suit and most editors agree. Unfortunately there is nothing in law that says three sources make it right, or six, or one hundred. Such "rules" are arbitrary and based on the fact that they have worked in the past, not on court interpretations of similar past cases.

The best material proof available would probably be a videotape of the incident you are describing with the subject as narrator. You will use virgin tape recorded once so that you cannot be accused of altering it.

Polaroid photos and a sworn confession made in front of several respected witnesses from different walks of life might also be good. However, such care in documentation is seldom taken when the experience is occurring.

The answer is to get all the facts you can in as many different forms as you can. A criminal case that has been resolved will leave an often extensive public records paper trail in the court storage system. You can interview the prosecutor and defense counsel, the convict, and, hopefully, the victim.

Personal matters are more complex. You have the statements of the person, his or her friends and acquaintances. You may have a diary or letters. There may be deeds of sale of a house or business. There may be corporate records. Any number of objects might exist and be available.

Whatever the case, your first job is to determine what facts you know about the person and the sources for your information. Then you must decide what is relevant.

Evaluating Material

There is no right way to evaluate material you have obtained. Everything is circumstantial. Ultimately you may have to go by your instincts, though first you must investigate everything.

For example, when writing the biography of a suburban Phoenix, Arizona, housewife who was arrested for a murder she did not commit, I found that one investigator was her strongest enemy. He warned the woman that he would see her in the gas chamber and, if you look at his court testimony, he seems to be convinced of her guilt. No problems so far.

Then came FBI files made public record and available through both the defense attorney's office and the use of the Freedom of Information Act. This time there were no accusations against the woman. All details seemed to point to either her husband or her brother. One memo concludes with a statement concerning the husband's alleged guilt and the fact that he is going to be arrested. And among these are references to reports by the primary investigator that indicate he shared these assumptions. Nothing was there indicating that the wife had any knowledge or involvement with the crime.

Suddenly there was an entirely different story emerging. Now I had the brother of the woman as a possible suspect and an investigator who said one thing in court, another thing in private memos.

The investigator was becoming a major character whose motivations were unknown and whose actions seemed in conflict. I personally felt that the woman had been set up as a means of forcing the hand of either her husband or her brother. I also recognized two other possibilities that were even worse. One was that the investigator was incompetent. The other was that the investigator wanted to be listed as having won the case and would do anything for a conviction, even home in on the wrong person.

There was more evidence than just the investigator's statements. There were witnesses who perjured themselves on the stand in order to gain a conviction (it took three trials to conclusively prove the woman's innocence). But the key witness perjured himself in his earliest statements that either were not cross-checked, or the lies, and they were ones which affected the entire credibility of the case, were not checked by the investigator.

Suddenly I had a fabulous story and a potentially serious libel allegation. I called the investigator and tape recorded his refusal to speak with me about the case or anything else in his life.

Then I gathered the transcripts from the three trials and noted the perjuries. I noted charges brought against the investigator by defense counsel as well as how he defended himself against those charges out of court. I showed what could have been checked right from the start and how easy it was to prove the information false. And I quoted the prosecutor as to why the case was valid enough to bring to trial.

The book carefully presented all the evidence involved and stated that the investigator refused to comment about the case. I pointed out the unanswered questions concerning his actions without accusing him of doing anything dishonest or improper. Where he looked bad, it was clear that there was no way to check beyond what had been done. And where he looked good, such information was included.

What was the outcome of the text? I was careful to not libel him, yet the weight of the documentation and his refusal to speak made him look bad. I was careful to show all the reasons why he might have felt that he was acting on the best available evidence. I was careful to show why his failure to act differently may have been for reasons that seemed valid at the time. There was nothing more that I could do to alter the image that he created by his refusal to speak with me and by the public records available.

On the other hand, suppose your subject says to you, "I don't remember much about that time period. I was an alcoholic then and constantly on a drunk."

Such a statement, made about the person by someone else, would be libelous without corroboration. But the statement made by the individual is not libelous. You may quote him directly and, if he later becomes embarrassed by the publicity that might result, you have done nothing wrong.

By contrast, there is a problem in generalizing about a situation even when the evidence indicates that a condition like alcoholism is present. For example, a murderer concerned in a book I'm working on has refused to call himself an alcoholic. However, he described a year in his life prior to the murder when he was drinking constantly. He talked about taking a can of beer the moment he awakened and drinking steadily until he went to bed. The only exceptions were days when he worked as an airplane pilot, yet he admitted that there were days then when he had to call in "sick."

He was describing what men and women in Alcoholics Anonymous and other such programs would call alcoholism. But because I am quoting him and he refused to use that term, I have to describe his drinking pattern as it was without putting a label on it that could be defamatory in his mind.

The situation does not change with historic figures. There have been cases of descendants bringing lawsuits because of the defamation of an individual. Yet always the truth, in this case through diaries and other writings, is a defense.

Public versus Private Figures

The term public figure is both difficult and easy to define. Some of the definitions are obvious. An entertainer is a public figure. He or she makes a living by being in the spotlight, whether on the stage, on radio, television, or in films. Likewise, a politician is a public figure. Even election to office requires being far more vulnerable and open than would normally be expected of anyone.

The deliberate use of the media to promote one's self and, at times, one's cause, can make you a public figure. As a writer, you become one at the very least when you start promoting your book, screen or stage play, or other creative works. Likewise someone who is deliberately active socially, such as the chairperson for community fund raisers or the promoter of events at country clubs, becomes a public figure. Yet the spouses of such people generally are not public figures. Likewise, someone who is a teacher may not fit the public figure category, even though a teacher regularly addresses large groups of individuals, but a professional lecturer would be considered a public figure.

There is also the question of when a public figure has a right to privacy. The courts have held that what a public figure does in restaurants, clubs, on the streets, and in similar areas where everyone is likely to have free access is fair game for writers and photographers. You can write about a public figure hugging and kissing someone in a restaurant who is not that person's spouse provided your report is accurate. Yet if you were to hide in a motel room closet or place hidden microphones in the person's bedroom in order to capture proof of an affair, you would be invading that individual's privacy.

No matter whether someone is a public figure or not, there are generally four ways in which you can be guilty of invading his or her privacy. The first is through intrusion. This means the placing of tape recorders or other equipment for listening, filming, or otherwise recording someone. Reporters who take hidden cameras or tape recorders into seemingly confidential locations for a story—

sneaking them into a private office or even into a home after agreeing to respect the home owner's privacy may constitute intrusion and thus an illegal invasion of privacy.

The difference is when you are invited into a private setting—home, office, etc.—specifically to take notes, write an article, research a book, or otherwise involve yourself in a commercial venture. Then whatever you witness is fair game and not libelous, again so long as it meets the proofs necessary for it to be the truth.

It has generally been held that anyone who commits a crime, is arrested, and goes on trial is a public figure, at least so far as your writing about the crime is concerned. When the person is convicted, anything in his or her life is fair game for a book. Yet this does not mean that those around that person are necessarily public figures. The backgrounds of the victims can be discussed. Any key people in the case, such as investigators, can be written about. Yet many people on the periphery, including family members with no connection to the crime, may have a right to be completely left alone. To seek information on them may be to violate their right to privacy.

It is doubtful that you will be involved with a story where misappropriation is a concern. This is most common with advertising agencies. However, it would be misappropriation if I claimed that a book subject should talk with me based on the endorsement of subjects of my work, especially since some of my biographies have been unauthorized. This would be presenting myself under false pretenses.

The third way is what is known as publicizing in a false light. This means that your material is knowingly inaccurate yet is not libelous. A typical example would be the biographer who creates incidents in childhood that make cute stories but that have no basis in fact. Many of the Reverend Weems' biographies, such as his life of Washington, fall into this category.

And finally there is the issue of the public disclosure of private and embarrassing facts. This is not an easy one to define for the courts, though fortunately it is usually not an issue.

The classic example would be the case of a woman who is a rape victim yet whose name and story never are in the paper. Her name is withheld from public records, yet somehow you find out who she is. You then print her name in a book about rape victims. Under such circumstances you would be in violation of the issue of public disclosure of private and embarrassing facts.

The exceptions to this are likely to be of concern for you. The first is where the person has done something in public in front of others and you are only reporting what went on in such circumstances. The second is where you are dealing with a public figure again acting in front of others. For example, while former First Lady Nancy Reagan's Hollywood romance with the late Robert Walker might be embarrassing in light of her present position, the fact that she was with him in public and her private behavior discussed by many living witnesses who were present would prevent this from fitting such a category.

The Private Person Connected with a Public Figure

The act of being caught up in history or even in the wake of a public person can affect what is and is not libel. For example, several years ago the head of a major industry sued for divorce. The divorce proceedings were public record when filed and some reporters thought they made for juicy reading. The industrial magnate accused his wife of adultery in a rather titillating statement that included a certain amount of kinky sex. She said that she was innocent of the charges, though she was willing to go along with getting the divorce. The fact that he could make such allegations was proof that the relationship had been shattered.

Eventually the wife brought a lawsuit against a publication, declaring the statement they had quoted to be libelous. She showed that she had proven in court that they were false, but the reporters said that she was a public figure going through a proceeding that was public record. They could print the charges so long as they also printed the outcome of the divorce proceedings. They also stated that she had no right to privacy in such a matter because she was a public figure, further reason for their printing their earlier statement.

The reporters lost.

The woman pointed out that she was not a public figure, though her husband certainly was. He had his own golf tournament, actively courted the media, and kept a high public profile. However, she showed that she did not participate in his public life, staying home or tending to private business of her own. Her absence was unique in her social set, often questioned by reporters, and probably one of the reasons he chose to divorce her. But regardless of the reasons, she was not a public figure.

Then the woman stated that she had proven the allegations made in the divorce proceedings to be false. Had the reporters done their job, they could have discovered the same thing. Yet they made no effort to call her for a statement. They simply printed the public record and the public record proved to be made up of false statements made by her then ex-husband.

Lawyers evaluating the judgment found that there were several things that should have been done to prevent the libel issue. The first was a limiting of what was quoted from the divorce proceedings to the simple statement that a divorce was about to take place. Had they wanted to quote general charges of adultery, they would have needed a statement from the wife concerning those charges. However, they had no right to detail erotic specifics that were unchecked and unproven (and ultimately shown to be false).

The reporters also could have waited until the divorce proceedings had taken place, then told the full story including the early charges in detail. The fact that she had been cleared would show her ex-husband in a bad light, all quite proper because the facts would be evident. It was their timing and their lack of effort to be objective, to check the allegations, and present a balanced article that was their undoing.

Oddly, had the wife been a public figure, the reporters might have been all right. At the worst, they may have been guilty of sloppy journalism.

New York Times v. Sullivan

Attorney Martin Garbus, a partner in the New York City law firm of Frankfurt, Garbus, Klein & Selz, is considered one of the leading experts on publishing and First Amendment issues. He has stressed that the standard for libel questions has been the case of *The New York Times v. Sullivan*. This case resulted in the decision that the libel laws of each state were subject to the federal Constitution. No state could create its own libel law that might inhibit someone's constitutional rights. A public official could sue someone in the media for libel only if the public official could show "actual malice" that Garbus has defined as "a knowledge of the falsity of a story or publication in reckless disregard of whether the story was true."

"Reckless disregard" can be looked at in a number of different ways. If someone receives extensive documentation concerning an allegedly corrupt public official, decides to write a story about the person, and calls for an interview with that official, in theory the reporter is trying to be fair. Now suppose that the official refuses an interview. The writer only has statements against the person but has made no effort to check them beyond trying to reach the subject. This could be construed as "reckless disregard" for the facts. On the other hand, if the writer is new, inexperienced, and untrained, the writer may not know what to do beyond trying to reach the subject for a balancing statement or explanation. Should the writer be responsible for the printing (he almost never is), there may be no malice involved and thus no libel.

On the other hand, suppose the writer knows that a story is not true or that it is patently outrageous. The story is about someone whose past behavior has been so shocking that he or she seems fair game for using the story that is no worse than other information that has come out before. And it is the kind of story people believe might be true (such as a womanizing politician allegedly having contracted a venereal disease when the writer knows that the person is in perfect health and his latest blood test came back without a problem). In such an instance, the writer will justifiably lose the libel suit.

Garbus warns that there are some risks of change within cases appearing before the Supreme Court. He points out that there seems a tendency by a majority of the court to one day allow a state's libel laws to take precedent over the national laws. This would be like the obscenity statutes that are based on community standards. Should this occur, a writer who meets the standards for Michigan and forty-eight other states, for example, might be successfully sued in Florida. This would be a dangerous eroding of our freedoms but fortunately has not yet occurred. We still must deal with the malice issue.

Garbus, in a friend of the court (amicus curiae) brief in the case of *David Price v. Viking Penguin, Inc.* and Peter Matthiessen, submitted on October 19, 1988, to the United States Court of Appeals (8th Circuit), quoted the following opinion that was the standard from which Sullivan evolved. The quote (*Whitney v. California*, 274 U.S. 357, 374-75 — 1927 — J. Brandeis concurring) stated:

"To reach sound conclusions on these matters we must bear in mind why a state is, ordinarily, denied the power to prohibit dissemination of social, economic and political doctrine which a vast majority of its citizens believes to be false and fraught with evil consequence.

"Those who won our independence believed that the final end of the state was to make men free to develop their faculties; and that in its government the deliberative forces should prevail over the arbitrary. They valued liberty both as an end and as a means. They believed that freedom to think as you will and to speak as you think are means indispensible to the discovery and spread of political truth; that without free speech and assembly discussion would be futile; that with them, discussion affords ordinarily adequate protection against the dissemination of noxious doctrine . . . the remedy to be applied is more speech, not enforced silence."

Absence of Malice

The issue of malice is probably the most critical factor in any libel case at the moment. It is hard for a biographer to not be biased. Something compels you to write about a person and that may be love, hate, hero worship, respect for the person's place in history, or any other number of reasons. Often there is a bias. Hitler is considered the most evil leader of the twentieth century. Mother Teresa is considered the most spiritually driven woman of faith, a potential future saint. Dr. Martin Luther King, Jr. began the drive that drastically reduced the effects of racial bias in our society. Charles Manson was the obsessed leader of a group of serial killers.

Research cannot have that bias. It is important to attempt to learn the truth, then relay it fairly and objectively, even when the truth goes against preconceived notions. Every effort must be made to let the person tell his or her own story. A lack of bias must exist in the actual writing regardless of your personal opinion or the opinion you hope your readers will express.

Many writers point to the fact that it is permissible to give one's opinion. This is true, but what they are not looking at are the circumstances surrounding the giving of an opinion. It is one thing to write for the Op/Ed page of a daily newspaper. This is a section meant for "opinion and editorial," the terms from which "Op/Ed" is derived. But an opinion piece in magazines and newspapers, or an opinion expressed editorially on radio and television, is different from an opinion expressed in a book. The length of the work is such that if a book is sold as a biography, it is expected to be properly researched. Let your opinion color what you say in a biography and you may have shown malice toward your subject.

Objectivity and truth without editorial comment will mean far more when protecting yourself against the allegation of malice than a belief that since opinion can be stated in the appropriate section of a newspaper, opinion in a book is not an act of bias. Play it straight, without malice, without letting your bias show through, and you will protect yourself from this aspect of a potential lawsuit.

The as-told-to autobiography holds slightly more perils because your subject may have no knowledge of the law and no interest in objectivity. "It's my opinion," the person may say. "Put it in that way. State, 'In my opinion . . .' That protects you and I'm certainly willing to pay any consequences for what's in the book."

Such statements come up with greater frequency than I would like and there are few ways to protect yourself from such an attitude. However, protect yourself you must, even though it usually means dominating an occasional section of the book you are writing.

For example, suppose you are writing the as-told-to autobiography of theatrical agent Boyce Braggart. He is talking about when he knew world-famous singer Tommy Tonsils when Tonsils was just another kid from Hoboken, New Jersey, trying to break into show business. He occasionally represented the young Tonsils, sending him to weddings, confirmations, and other gatherings, as well as getting him low-paying jobs singing in sleazy nightclubs. "He was a thief, that punk," Braggart tells you. "Always chiselin', always taking stuff from the club tables and back rooms that he could hock for a few bucks. And worse than the stealing was the fact that he never paid me my share. He owed me 10 percent of everything, but the smart mouth only said I should follow him when he went to the toilet so I could get my percentage of that. Hell, I used to call him the thief of Hoboken."

The trouble is that Tonsils was never arrested when growing up. You may have reason to dislike Tommy Tonsils, but you know that what you are hearing is probably an exaggeration.

By contrast, suppose your as-told-to autobiography is with J. Kindly Grandfather, the evening news television network anchor who is considered the most watched and trusted news person in America. Millions regard an event of the day of no importance at all unless the newscaster mentions it on his show, the most popular in the nation. And suppose he says much the same thing about Tonsils.

The facts remain the same. Tonsils was never arrested. You are dealing with opinion. And both subjects want you to write what they have said.

Now the malice issue is a serious one. Boyce Braggart is the lesser concern. If you are writing in the first person, and if you have Boyce stating from the outset that the book is filled with outrageous opinions no one should take too seriously, you probably can quote him. This probably would be a little like comedian Don Rickles who made his living heckling both average people and name entertainers. His comments were outrageous, exaggerations at the very least, outright falsehoods at the worst, yet everyone knew that he was not serious.

The important points are twofold here. One is that Boyce is making it clear throughout the book that his statements are often exaggerations and meant to not be taken as fact. You may even intersperse with serious sections that are so obviously straightforward that the contrast is evident to everyone.

The second point is that Boyce Braggart is a theatrical agent. He is someone who is a lesser known of show business, the appeal in his story being his ability to drop "names" in an interesting and amusing manner from his personal experience.

By contrast, J. Kindly Grandfather is a man known by millions for his integrity and honesty. This is the person who delivers the news each night. The fact that he may be reading from a teleprompter has nothing to do with the public's faith in his words. He is truth personified.

Now suppose you use the same approach in Grandfather's first-person account as you plan to use for Braggart. In all likelihood you would be struck with an unwinnable libel suit.

What is the difference? The reputation of Grandfather. His words will be given far greater credibility than those of others. He cannot make outrageous statements about someone's character unless he declares each statement to be a joke. However, in the example just given, a joke would not be appropriate. People will tend to automatically believe anything that J. Kindly Grandfather says, giving him less ability to exaggerate or provide opinions without risk of a successful libel suit.

The reason I am providing this example is to show you that the issue of libel can be highly subjective. As a result, it is extremely important that you consult an attorney specializing in libel and First Amendment issues if there is any question. Such attorneys are usually best found through university law schools (many top professors do consulting work on the side) and through state chapters of the American Civil Liberties Union (ACLU). Few lawyers in private practice have the background and expertise to help you without extensive research into the field at your expense. Professors involved with First Amendment issues keep up to date on the various related court cases, new laws, and the interpretations thereof. Attorneys in private practice who handle this work, such as New York's Martin Garbus, are few in number and usually work either near the book-publishing centers or in Hollywood where some of these issues are tackled by the movie industry.

When Should You Worry About Libel?

There are a number of circumstances when you need to be alert to the libel issues. The following is a general list covering many of the most important areas.

1. Criminal allegations. A person who has been indicted and convicted of a crime is a criminal. A person who has been indicted but not tried is an alleged criminal based on the case being brought against him. A person who has been indicted and acquitted is as innocent as someone who has never been through the justice system at all.

Sometimes you encounter a story where you find that someone has been committing crimes or is guilty of improper behavior. Document the person's actions without saying that he or she is guilty of anything. Just give the facts and make certain you can prove them through eyewitness accounts, documents, taped interviews, and/or other evidence that both directly relates and could be used in a court of law. Then let your reader come to his or her own conclusions.

2. Explicit sex discussion. This falls into two categories. One is the unauthorized biography and the other is the as-told-to book. Anyone can discuss their own intimate life. However, discussing other participants, including someone's spouse, without their agreement may be libelous.

For example, the late actor Peter Lawford enjoyed indulging in sex with two women. When writing his biography, I could quote the notes he left behind when planning his book prior to his death, and I could quote his widow with whom I worked. But I learned the names of some of the most famous, respected, and beautiful women in Hollywood who had participated. The widow was a witness and, at times, a participant when she was desensitized through extreme drug abuse to what she felt was a disgusting action. But there were no others and quoting the names would not have done anything except increase the "sleaze." I also could have been accused of libel with no recourse because the only living witness would have been perceived as biased since she would have been a codefendant.

A man or woman can talk about an unusual sex life. However, when it comes to naming partners to what others might consider unnatural or improper acts, you are risking libel.

The same is true with sexual preference. An individual may admit to being homosexual, but do not name the same sex partner without permission. This is especially true if the partner is bisexual.

3. Causes of death. The age of AIDS has made this an extra burden for a writer. There was a time when the major concern was whether or not someone would be embarrassed by a suicide in the family. Now the issue of AIDS is the greatest concern.

It is important to make your decision based on the autopsy report and the information released by the individual. If the autopsy reads that the person died of a rare form of cancer you know is normally found only in adults with AIDS, quote the stated cause of death. Don't hint at the AIDS in the manner I just did because you may find that the person truly had that cancer and not AIDS.

An AIDS cover-up is fair to discuss, though. The entertainer Liberace was homosexual and known for his orgies on the road. Yet he kept his public and private lives so separate that his AIDS was not known until after his death. While he was dying from the illness, an attempt at a cover-up was made, a story being released that he was suffering from the ill effects of too fast a weight loss as a result of a watermelon diet he had tried. This patently ridiculous cover-up is now part of the history of Liberace and belongs in any biography written about his life and death.

Likewise the attempt by Rock Hudson to conceal his AIDS, potentially risking the health of female costars with whom he had passionate kissing scenes, is also "fair game" and not libelous. His actions were known, a former lover proving that he was also put at risk.

More subtle are situations that are tragedies. For example, one director, formerly a television star, faces the loss of his entire family from AIDS. His one child just died and his other child is dying. His wife may also die and, if she does, he may be next.

To avoid a libel suit with the director, the full circumstances must be related. The wife contracted AIDS from contaminated blood given to her following surgery and while she was nursing her newborn. The child contracted AIDS through the milk, then their next child contracted it in the womb. The wife shows no signs of the AIDS virus, nor does the director. But there is a good chance that the wife will come down with it and she may have passed it on to her husband. It is an American tragedy that has nothing to do with homosexuality or drug abuse. A hospital made a mistake and an entire family may be destroyed because of it. To not go into any more details than a mention that AIDS is the cause of death would be to risk a successful libel suit in today's climate concerning the disease.

4. Past or present employers or employees. There is a perceived bias on the part of an employee toward an employer or an employer toward an employee. The nature of the relationship is such that this can occur. Yet former employees or employers, as well as former spouses, make great sources for unauthorized biographies and there is where care must be taken.

Whenever you can presume bias, such as with a former spouse, you have to be unusually careful. Oddly I have found that former spouses and lovers are among the most objective individuals when I am writing an unauthorized biography, especially if they have been separated for a few years. However, since the relationship usually ended in pain, and since both sides often have said things they later regretted, there will be a perception of bias.

5. Failure to check seemingly secondary facts. The last major libel risk comes when you get sloppy on seemingly minor matters. For example, you fail to check the exact spelling of someone's first and last names. Is John Smith actually spelled Jon Smith by the person you are mentioning on page 367 of your manuscript? Or is he Jahn? What about Smyth? Smythe?

Or perhaps you get dates wrong. Or your subject talks about appearing on the "Ed Sullivan Show" and, though he or she actually appeared on the program, the time period you were given was six months after Sullivan died.

Many of these points will be quite minor. Few people will be aware that a mistake was made. Unfortunately such mistakes on little matters call into question allegations of mistakes made with larger issues. There can be a presumption of a libelous error just because you have not done an effective job checking smaller matters.

Libel Insurance

Libel insurance is available for writers, though the fees are high and the requirements quite intense. There are blanket policies sold for high fees. Less expensive is libel insurance per book because the insurance company's lawyers will often review your documentation to such a degree that when the policy is issued, the company already knows that there is little chance of losing a suit.

Some book publishers now pay for libel insurance for their authors. Most do not. While it is theoretically a good idea for a contemporary unauthorized biography, the cost is prohibitive for almost every writer. You are best off documenting your work with enough care for details that you do feel comfortable with any possible challenge to the integrity of your work.

Libel is a constant concern for biographers. Be certain of your facts. Keep copies of all documents. Make tape recordings where appropriate. And consult an attorney knowledgeable about libel and the First Amendment when in doubt. Volunteer Lawyers for the Arts will work with you for minimal fees. You can contact them at the following telephone numbers: Bay Area Lawyers for the Arts — (415) 775-7200 in San Francisco; Lawyers for the Creative Arts — (312) 944-2787 in Chicago; Volunteer Lawyers for the Arts — (212) 977-9270 in New York. A little care will keep you from ever having to worry about losing a libel suit.

The moral and ethical issues are unfortunately not so clear-cut. What if the individual lies? What if the individual wants to twist history for his or her own ends? What if the person wants to exaggerate what happened or ignore key elements of the story?

There is no right or wrong answer here. The writers interviewed for this book had comments ranging from "I never had to give it any thought" to "I'd take the money and run." None had faced it in real life and, perhaps, most writers never do.

The most common area for a subject to be self-serving is when that person has or aspires to high political office. Richard Nixon wrote the book *Six Crises*, a book President Eisenhower felt was self-serving and inaccurate in its account of the Middle East conflict. Eisenhower's own autobiography fell short of calling his former vice-president a liar, but the implication was there. Knowing this, it can be presumed that further autobiographies by Nixon would be equally self-serving and incorrect. Should a "ghost" or cowriter cross-check what was being stated and demand that the facts be made right?

There was a time when I would have said that this should be done without question. Then I began watching incidents that were taking place in the nation. The Reverend Jesse Jackson, while running for President in 1987 and 1988, claimed at one time to have cradled the head of the dying Martin Luther King, Jr. in his lap after Dr. King was shot by a sniper. There are dozens of photographs of the incident, all of them proving that Jackson's memory of the event is incorrect at best, a deliberate lie at worst. Yet the fact that he would say such a thing in disregard of the obvious evidence to the contrary reveals more about his character than if the statement was not made. Thus if I was working with him on his autobiography and he asked to include that statement, I would do it. The false claim would do more to reveal the inner man than a straight recitation of the facts.

The same is true with the autobiographies of presidents who have been notorious. I would rather record the incorrect information they would like in the book, if any and if nonlibelous, than to correct them with the truth. Their statements will be checked against the facts by any serious reporter, author, or researcher so I would not be changing history. And I would be allowing them to be judged based on their actions, not a sanitized version of the real person.

This is quite different from my attitude when writing a biography, whether authorized or not. A biography is my work, and my reputation is on the line. If someone wants me to lie on their behalf, that is fine. It is also my job to not only quote what the person wants said, but also to counterpoint that statement with the facts. I do not deny them their statements. I simply meet a higher obligation to be certain that the truth is included at the same place so the reader can make his or her own judgment about the incident and the person involved.

Remember that this is true even with an authorized biography. Publishers know that when they see a joint byline on a book, only one person wrote it (there are exceptions but they are rare). They hold the writer accountable, though not to the degree that they do when only the author's name is on the jacket. Thus it would be ethically wrong as an authorized biographer to simply quote what the person says, regardless of truth. Either work together or be scrupulously accurate, regardless of the reaction of the person who has commissioned the personal work. Otherwise your reputation will be damaged.

Parson Weems and his ilk would not write nonfiction today with the liberties they took and ever sell more than one book. No matter what your current plans, there is a chance that you will be doing far more writing in this field than you can imagine. Avoid actions that will cause a publisher to shy away from you.

Ten Ethical Questions Before Writing
Before writing any biography, there are a few rules you should follow to ensure fairness and objectivity.

1. Never presume anything about an individual or an event until you have checked all aspects of it. You almost always start a biography with a bias for or against an individual. You also make assumptions about their skills based on their accomplishments. However, those are in hindsight.

For example, most people know that Napoleon was defeated at Waterloo. But the biographer must know that Napoleon actually won. The British were in retreat when they realized that Napoleon's army was also fleeing. The British leaders instantly recognized that Napoleon had misjudged his situation. They took advantage of that fact, regrouping, attacking, and forcing him into exile. Had Napoleon not misunderstood what was happening, he would have won. And that failed awareness was a fatal flaw in his character and leadership that has to be addressed.

It does not matter if the truth somehow shatters your preconceived notions about the person. What is important is that you find out as much as you can before you start writing, accepting the good with the bad, checking both to make certain they are accurate.

2. Recognize that all actions by an individual shape their character. Covering up aspects of history because they are unpleasant not only weakens your book, it also prevents full understanding of the man or woman who is your subject. Human weakness can be as much a way to show the true greatness of positive endeavors as can human strength. Even the Bible reveals all aspects of man, from the fall of Adam and Eve to the biography of King David. The latter is considered by religious leaders to have been most favored with God, yet there was a time in his life when he sent his girlfriend's husband to the front lines to ensure his death in battle.

3. Define your readers. Most biographies will be aimed toward a large audience. Sometimes this will be for adults, other times for children or young adults. At still other times it might be for members of a religious group. The greater the audience, the fewer constraints you will have. However, as you have seen in the chapter on writing biographies for children and young adults, publishers of such books require as much honesty, though less intimate detail, than publishers of adult books.

4. What is the value of the information in question? Are you including details because they are titillating and you feel that a little sex, sin, or sleaze will sell more books? Has the subject changed radically so that by showing the extremes of his or her personality, you are revealing the greatness the person has achieved or the depths to which the subject has degenerated? Will the details provide a better understanding of an era? of a profession or lifestyle? Of influences that may affect current actions that would otherwise be overlooked?

Does the information provide an insight into other characters within the book? For example, when I wrote the Peter Lawford biography, the information about John Kennedy provided deeper insight into the emotional child abuse within the Kennedy family; the character of Robert Kennedy; the relationship of Jacqueline Kennedy Onassis to her father, Black Jack Bouvier; and the tragic life and death of Marilyn Monroe. To reduce or eliminate portions of the Kennedy story would be to limit the ability to give the reader an understanding of other extremely important people within the book.

Always remember that a story taken out of context is not the same as the story within the book. Sometimes it stands alone as a fascinating piece of reporting. At other times such isolation gives it an unpleasant twist that it did not have within the book. You must look at it in relation to the whole, not in isolation as may be done by the critics.

5. Who will be hurt by the revelations? This is a difficult question to answer. One man was worried about what his children would think when they learned he had been a career criminal. They proved delighted, bragging about his colorful past and wondering why he never told them. And these were honest, law-abiding, upstanding young men and women who would never consider committing the crimes he had committed.

In another instance, a mother asked me to not write a book because she did not want her teenaged daughter being hurt. I was also concerned about that, yet the story I was telling might ultimately send the woman to jail for her part in a murder. Without the book, she would go unpunished and, for reasons too complex to discuss here, there would be no way of proving with certainty whether or not she was involved without writing it.

6. If the material is not used, will the book be incomplete? Seriously weakened? Inaccurate? Leave grounds for misunderstanding the true story of the subject?
7. Have you carefully checked your facts? Do you feel that you can document everything that you have stated? Are those documents at hand? Can you make copies for the publisher's attorneys if necessary?
8. Does anyone whose statements you feel are valid contradict the information you want to use? It may be necessary to include the counterstatements in the interest of fairness and accuracy.
9. Are you comfortable with your decision to use the material? Is your attitude one of, "This is important for the reader's understanding"? Or is your attitude, "Wait until this hits the stands. I'll get rich with all the nasty scandals I'm revealing"? As a general rule you will find that what you do for the sake of the reader is the correct approach. What you do for per-

sonal gain, whether for money or fame, is probably the wrong approach.

10. Are you willing to decline to continue the biography if writing it accurately and effectively means writing it in a way with which you will not be comfortable in the future?

Once you have weighed these ten questions, it is time to move forward. We writers are always going to be subject to criticism. We also have to face the fact that the longer our careers, the more we will face the consequences of actions taken when we were inexperienced. But if you address the moral and ethical concerns at the start, you will find that should you decide to go ahead with the biography in the manner in which it should be written, you will always be comfortable with that decision, regardless of critics.

NINE

Writing the Biography

The Beginning

> When my mother was pregnant with me, she told me later, a party of hooded Ku Klux Klan riders galloped up to our home in Omaha, Nebraska, one night. Surrounding the house, brandishing their shotguns and rifles, they shouted for my father to come out. My mother went to the front door and opened it. Standing where they could see her pregnant condition, she told them that she was alone with her three small children, and that my father was away, preaching in Milwaukee. The Klansmen shouted threats and warnings at her that we had better get out of town because the "good Christian white people" were not going to stand for my father's "spreading trouble" among the "good" Negroes of Omaha with the "back to Africa" preachings of Marcus Garvey.
>
> — Opening paragraph of *The Autobiography of Malcom X*, "ghostwritten" by Alex Haley (Grove Press, Inc., New York, 1965)

Openings. They are perhaps the hardest part of any book but they are especially important with a biography. How do you draw someone into a life? How do you get the person to read a book about someone who is so famous that they may feel there is nothing new to be learned, or so obscure that only a fascinating beginning can draw the reader into the story?

Alex Haley's ghostwritten book *The Autobiography of Malcolm X* typifies some of the best writing in the biographical field. The book was released in 1965, an epilogue having to be added because of the subject's murder in February of 1965 by members of the Black Muslim group for which he was once a major spokesman and leadership symbol.

On a superficial level, anyone can appreciate the opening of this book. It is a dramatic, exciting incident told in fewer than two hundred words.

First we get a sense of the times in which Malcolm X (Malcolm

Little) was born. Omaha, Nebraska, is considered a progressive community today, as it was when this book was written. The people are cosmopolitan, sophisticated, and while Omaha is not seen as a miniature version of such truly international cities as New York, Chicago, and Los Angeles, it is not a city where people think of the Ku Klux Klan. White people in Omaha do not ride horses, carry shotguns, burn crosses, and threaten decent citizens. It doesn't happen. It isn't done. And yct it was.

But there is more than a cultural shock borne of looking back on a city that had matured in its race relations and attitudes toward violence. Much information is provided here. Malcolm Little's father was a minister and a spokesperson for the back-to-Africa movement of Marcus Garvey. The son was obviously born into controversy and violence. He was also born to strong parents, including a mother who had the courage to stand alone in the face of what could have been her death.

For those who are not familiar with Malcolm X, a brief background is important. He was a man who was brilliant, handsome, and courageous. His early years were spent as the street hustler, Detroit Red. He was in and out of jail and could easily have been killed by the police or one of the pimps, dope dealers, or thieves who were a part of his world. Instead, he not only survived, he became a part of the Black Muslim movement headed by Elijah Muhammad, a former con man. The Black Muslim movement was a racist variation of the Islamic religion, one that was frequently denounced for its corrupted teachings at the same time as it was being embraced by disenfranchised blacks. The organization demanded strict adherence to ethical standards that improved the lives of many of the followers. It provided the members a sense of self-respect, frequent economic gain by encouraging the establishment of small businesses, and better health by insisting that their diets improve. Yet it also talked of the white devil and fomented race hatred, something quite contrary to the Islamic faith as followed by millions of people of all colors throughout the world.

Malcolm X was a fiery spokesperson, a charismatic leader, who had a way of telling the truth about society. He was often misunderstood, such as when President Kennedy was assassinated and he stated that "the chickens have come home to roost." He was speaking of the fact that people who use violence against others often become the targets of violence themselves. The assassination occurred at a time when the civil rights movement was still in its relative infancy. Voter registration workers of both colors were being tortured and murdered in the rural south. It was a crime for a black person to sit at a lunch counter and order a meal in some parts of the country. Segregation was rampant, blacks and whites often facing radically different standards of justice. And Malcolm X was commenting on the tragic irony of the Kennedy assassination in such a climate.

The greatness of Malcolm X came not through his work for the Black Muslim movement but because of his concern for all blacks and his devotion to the Islamic faith. Shortly before his death he came to recognize the good and bad in all men. He turned against the racial divisiveness of the Black Muslim movement, made a pilgrimage to the holy city of Mecca, and began talking about brotherly love. The color of a man's skin no longer mattered to Malcolm X, only what was in his heart. It was a message quite different from the one he had been preaching and he drew far greater audiences than in the past. His words touched universal nerves and threatened the leadership of the extremist Black Muslim movement. He had to be assassinated or he was likely to be a uniting force in ways that would seriously deplete Elijah Muhammad's following.

It was the willingness to stand up to whatever establishment he felt was wrong that made Malcolm X almost a cult figure in a positive sense. He overcame poverty. He overcame an early life of crime. And he overcame a racist philosophy without ever losing his idealism. He was a self-made leader who, in all likelihood, would have had as positive an impact on American society as Rev. Dr. Martin Luther King, Jr., had he only lived a few years longer.

That is the Malcolm X history. At the time the as-told-to autobiography was released, Malcolm X was still a controversial figure. John Kennedy was recently assassinated. Alabama Governor George Wallace was still vowing to not be "out niggered" in Alabama politics. Civil rights violations were routine. And radical black groups such as the Black Panthers were raising the image of guerrilla warfare on inner-city streets.

The radical blacks were curious about Malcolm X. Many liberal blacks and whites wanted to know who he was. But there was an even larger market of ordinary people who wondered about this man, wondered if they should read the autobiography of so controversial a figure in so turbulent a period of American history. The opening paragraph was, in a sense, meant for them.

Taking another look at that paragraph, there are many clues to Malcolm's character laid before the reader. Marcus Garvey was a black man who had founded the Universal Negro Improvement Association (UNIA). Working from his New York headquarters, Garvey believed that the way for American Negroes to improve their existence was to return to Africa, their homeland. It was a belief that appealed to many blacks, especially since they perceived an economic impact that would plunge the United States into financial chaos. Blacks frequently worked menial tasks that whites depended upon to maintain the quality of their lives — garbage disposal, cleaning women, laborers, etc. They also spent a disproportionate share of their income, a fact that would remove billions of dollars from the economy if they left.

The problem with Garvey's idea was that most people did not want to return to the homeland of their ancestors. They were Americans, many tracing their roots to Colonial America. No matter how cruel the nation had been to them, it was the only culture they knew, understood, and desired. They wanted to improve their existence in the United States, not travel to a nation where not even the language would be familiar.

And so in one paragraph the reader is not only drawn into a dramatic period of history, he or she is also given an instant understanding of influences on Malcolm X's character. The reader is introduced to turbulent times, courageous parents, and a father who was both a preacher and a proponent of the back-to-Africa movement. It is a brilliant opening at any time. Considering the period of history during which the book reached the stores, it is no wonder that it became an immediate best seller.

Sometimes the opening of a biography establishes the bias of the biographer as well. Yet this is only learned when comparing biographies of the same individual by two different writers. For example, one of the more complex and fascinating individuals to develop the film industry was Schmuel Gelgfisz, a Polish Jew, whose name was changed to Samuel Goldfish after he reached America. Eventually he took the name Samuel Goldwyn and became head of Metro-Goldwyn-Mayer, one of the largest and most successful of the Hollywood studios. Among the books written about Goldwyn, two of the most respected are *Goldwyn: A Biography* by A. Scott Berg, and *The Search for Sam Goldwyn: A Biography* by Carol Easton. They open as follows:

> In 1947, a handful of Hollywood's royalty attended a dinner party given by Mr. and Mrs. Samuel Goldwyn in their sixteen-room home in Beverly Hills, just down the road from Pickfair and adjacent to the William Randolph Hearst estate. The five-acre Goldwyn spread contained all the obligatory Hollywood status symbols: swimming pool, tennis courts, manicured gardens and, as an added touch of opulence (an anniversary gift from Mrs. Goldwyn to her husband), croquet courts.
>
> The menu, planned by Mrs. Goldwyn, was elegant; the wines, selected by Mrs. Goldwyn, superb. Every detail was

first class, just like a Goldwyn movie. The party broke up around eleven. Getting into her car, one of the guests realized she'd left her gloves in the house; her husband, a director, went back to retrieve them. Passing the dining room doorway, the director got a rare glimpse of the real Sam Goldwyn: alone in the room, he was carefully pouring the wine left in the glasses back into a wine bottle.

Goldwyn had left the Warsaw ghetto at the age of eleven; but the ghetto never left Goldwyn.

— Opening of *The Search for Sam Goldwyn: A Biography* by Carol Easton (Quill Books, William Morrow & Company; New York, 1975)

Samuel Goldwyn was not born on August 27, 1882.

For most of his life he swore it was his day of birth, but both the name and the date were fabrications. He promulgated other distortions of the truth as well, liberties he took for dramatic effect. He spent years covering his tracks, erasing those details of his origins that embarrassed him. The reason, he revealed to a psychotherapist at the pinnacle of his career, was that ever since childhood he "wanted to be somebody." Starting at an early age, Samuel Goldwyn invented himself.

— Opening of *Goldwyn: A Biography* by A. Scott Berg (Alfred A. Knopf, New York, 1989)

For those familiar with the Goldwyn biographies, the Berg book is known to be the more accurate, though this is not because he was a better researcher. The Easton biography was written using interviews and available sources at the time. Berg had many similar resources, but he was also the first person to be given access to all of the Goldwyn family papers. He had material that had been unavailable to all previous researchers. Thus where there is a conflict of facts, dates, etc., the Berg book is considered the authority. Yet aside from that, notice the ways in which the writers chose to begin Goldwyn's story.

Berg grabs the reader's attention with the story of a man who created a myth. He tells the reader that no matter what you may have read, no matter what you think you know, it is probably not the truth. Sam Goldwyn was a self-made man in the most extreme manner possible. He fabricated his entire life.

Easton is drawn to quite a different experience. Her father was a Hollywood agent who, she claims, felt that he was a failure because he never made great wealth. By contrast, Goldwyn became rich but managed to isolate himself from reality. The attitudes of the two different biographers created quite different books in tone from the same facts, yet both are interesting from the start. The major difference is that Easton made herself a character in the book, describing her personal search for the real Goldwyn, while Berg used the Goldwyn papers, interviews, and other resources for the story.

A radically different type of pairing of openings comes with biographies of the late actor Errol Flynn. There has been extensive controversy about his life to such a degree that the public demand for work about him is unabated despite several best-selling biographies and a ghosted autobiography. The most recent is the work in progress (at this writing) by his daughter, Rory.

Charles Higham wrote the most controversial work, alleging Nazi connections and bisexuality. But before the controversy, he chose a quite different technique to introduce Flynn. He started by recreating Hobart, Tasmania, at the time of Errol's birth. He wrote:

> Picture a city some seventy years ago: the last great British port before the South Pole. A city of sixty-five thousand souls, a harbor town, filled with the sound of foghorns or ship's whistles; alive with sparkling sunshine or black with the long winter rains; swept by the terrible winds called the roaring forties.
>
> The architecture is a dour impersonation of England's: red brick houses with eaves and white-painted windowsills frowning on the clear Prussian blue or profound gloom of the harbor. Church bells and gardens and dark green lawns are forlorn echoes of a faraway home. It is a cozy colonial bulwark against the knowledge of remoteness. The heart aches for originals. Houses are built, lawns are groomed, businesses are attended, and beer is drunk. Steak and eggs are breakfasted upon. It seems a northern life. But there are strange trees, threatening bushes, birds which are too bright and exotic to fit in . . .
>
> — Opening from *Errol Flynn: The Untold Story*
> by Charles Higham (Doubleday & Company, Inc.;
> Garden City, New York; 1980

The smoke of battle was all about me. I was with Pickett at his final charge at Gettysburg. Men were dying all around. I might die. Ninety thousand of Lee's men had been at Chambersburg shortly before, and now they and thousands of others were massed opposite the Union troops. Scores of thousands lay over the battlefield—forever. The noise was overpowering. Shell explosions raged in my ears and I couldn't breathe.

The smoke from my own cigarettes—I had inhaled five

or six full cigarettes in the last twenty minutes — mingled with the smoke of the scene as Pickett yelled, "Charge!" I was writing the life story of William Henry and Fanny Seward and the death and destruction all about me in my kitchen where I worked was horrible. Would the Union win or wouldn't it?

The phone rang.

I staggered from my typewriter, breathless, asphyxiated by the Gettysburg smoke and a half pack of Camels.
— Opening of *Errol Flynn: A Memoir* by Earl Conrad
(Dodd, Mead & Company, New York, 1978)

This time the contrast is between a writer who attempts to recreate the environment in which Flynn was born with a writer who makes himself a major character. Conrad is writing a personal memoir with his opening, bringing the reader into his own world as that of a writer. All of us know what it is like to try and project ourselves into another time, another place, whether we are writing fiction or nonfiction. But I doubt that the average person who does not write, either for personal pleasure or as at least a partial source of income, would understand. Thus, though unusual, it seems a weaker opening that may be more intriguing for other writers than the general public.

The description of the town where Flynn was born fits into the chronological type of approach that is one of the easiest and most logical structures for the biography. I used a variation in one of my as-told-to autobiographies concerning a psychiatrist who became a specialist in the field of multiple personality. That book began:

Santa Cruz, California, was a small coastal community when I established my psychiatric practice there in the early 1960s. The few thousand year-round residents were mostly quiet people whose main source of livelihood came from the summer tourists who flocked to the area's high mountains and towering redwood trees. The community was barely touched by the riots and dissension that rocked the rest of the state during that era of political and social upheaval. The residents were friendly and more concerned with day-to-day living than with issues such as the Vietnam War and racial integration. It was an ideal place to settle and raise a family. And the psychiatric problems I encountered there were, for the most part, fairly routine.
— Opening of *Minds in Many Pieces:*
The Making of a Very Special Doctor
by Ralph Allison, M.D. with Ted Schwarz
(Rawson, Wade Publishers, Inc.; New York, 1980)

In the case of the Allison book, I wanted to show a contrast between a quiet doctor trying to raise a family in a college town with the extremely dramatic mental illness that is multiple personality. His life was fairly routine, though the case histories provided the book's fascination.

By contrast, I spent weeks trying to find an opening for a book about one of Allison's patients. I needed something to grab the reader and get the person intensely involved with the book. After several days of thought, I came up with:

> One afternoon when I was three years old, I lay down to take my nap. I didn't awaken for forty years. No one knew I was sleeping, because during that time four different people took my place.
>
> I was a multiple personality.
>
> —Opening of *The Five of Me*
> by Henry Hawksworth with Ted Schwarz
> (Henry Regnery Company, Chicago, 1977)

There is no right way to open your biography, the only "wrong" way being an approach that does not cause the reader to turn the page. Sometimes you are presenting the essence of the book, at other times a fascinating anecdote that draws the reader into the text. And at still others you may be starting with the birth and working forward.

Searching for Anecdotes

I am a firm believer in not starting the biography until everything is known. This is not to say that I always wait to begin writing until the research is complete. Sometimes an aspect of the book stands alone, allowing a chapter to be written out of context. This approach saves time, especially if you are working with a word processor or computer where material can be electronically manipulated as the book is being written. Typewriters require you to do extensive retyping that computers do not, a definite advantage, but you can work both ways.

For example, I am currently writing the biography of an artist whose work was used to help promote the Atchison, Topeka & Santa Fe Railroad's western expansion. One of the chapters deals with the history of railroad travel, including the horrors of railroad dining before a man named Fred Harvey revolutionized railroad food service. I have no idea in which chapter the Harvey story belongs, but I have all the research completed for that section and am writing it while researching the rest of the book. Then, when I actually begin putting things into context, I will move the chapter to wherever is appropriate.

Generally you will find that you are able to collect anecdotes along the way while looking for whatever will be best for the book. For example, although I did not know where I would begin the book *Power and Greed: Inside the Teamsters Empire of Corruption,* I knew that everything would be based around Allen Friedman, the subject of the book. As he talked, I noted which stories might be fun to have for the opening or in the first chapter.

For example, one day, while discussing his work as a "slugger" or muscle man for Jimmy Hoffa, Allen mentioned his mother being a high stakes gambler. He talked about how she and her friends would often have two thousand dollars in the pot, and this was in the early 1920s when such a sum was as much as some people earned in a year.

As Allen talked of this woman, he mentioned her strength as well as her love of cards. He explained that she was having a high stakes poker game the day she went into labor. She excused herself from the table, went upstairs to her bedroom, gave birth to Allen, rested for a couple of hours, and then returned to the game. She wasn't about to let a little thing like childbirth keep her away from what might become a winning hand. I found the story delightful and knew that it might make a good lead.

Likewise when researching Peter Lawford, I came across the tragic story of his birth. His mother was married to a colonel and having an affair with General Sir Sidney Lawford. She became pregnant by the general and let the colonel know that their relationship was over. Shattered, the colonel summoned his soon-to-be ex-wife to his quarters where he met her in full dress uniform, though wearing no shoes. Instead he was holding a shotgun against the floor, his toe near the trigger. As his wife watched in horror, the colonel saluted her, then used his toe to pull the trigger, killing him before her eyes. His wife, eight-and-a-half months pregnant with another man's child, was emotionally shattered and came to hate the baby in her womb she almost lost from the trauma.

This story was more horrible than the first, yet it was dramatic enough that I knew I needed to keep it in mind. Again it comes early in the biography, though I did not use it as the lead.

By contrast, I started John DeLorean's autobiography with a letter he wrote to his lawyer the night before he flew to Los Angeles where he was arrested in the midst of a supposed drug deal. The letter showed that he believed he was going to meet the Mafia. He thought he would be murdered and was traveling to assure the safety of his wife and children. Then, after introducing the letter and his subsequent arrest, I went back to a chronological telling of his story.

Why the difference in approach since all three books were written chronologically? It was because I felt that the DeLorean book buyers were likely to be hostile to him. They would want to know whether he was innocent or guilty of the charges for which he had recently been acquitted. In fact, many of the potential readers might not buy the book if they were fairly convinced of his guilt. There was vicious talk that he may have somehow bribed the jury that freed him, a charge that stemmed from the limited coverage of key witnesses who admitted that DeLorean's arrest was essentially a setup. I felt the need to defuse public hostility or risk not selling the book.

Stephen Singular, the author of *Talked to Death: The Life and Murder of Alan Berg* (Beech Tree Books, William Morrow & Co.; New York; 1987), faced a different concern at the opening of his book on the murder of the Denver, Colorado, talk show host. Neither the subject, Alan Berg, nor the murder were household words, though the death did make the national media. It was unusual for an on-air talk show host to be attacked by irate fans, much less murdered. Thus while the story was fascinating, the man had to be recreated. The first chapter became a vehicle for recreating Berg in a way that would grab the reader's attention. In addition to general details about his life and career at the time of his death, there were some anecdotes that would draw the reader's interest. Among these was the mention of a 1970s' contest in Denver to determine the public's most liked and most disliked media personality. Berg won both titles.

At the end of the chapter, following the murder, Singular further fleshes out attitudes toward Berg by quoting Don Mulnix, chief of detectives for the Denver Police Department. Mulnix was asked about any suspects for the murder. He was quoted as saying, "There are at least two million suspects. Anybody within the sound of his voice might have had a motive for killing him."

Thus Singular takes longer to set the story because he has more areas to overcome. Berg was not a household name outside his broadcast region prior to his death. The man, his work, and the area from which his show could be heard were all relatively obscure compared with stories where the subject is known to most of the nation. He uses a chapter to set the scene where others were able to use a paragraph or two to grab their reader's attention. And this is the reason I say that you use whatever works, usually waiting until the research for the book is finished before attempting to find the best opening. Sometimes your original idea is the one with which you end. At other times it will be something unexpected, an anecdote or quote, that seems the perfect way to begin.

Flashbacks

The DeLorean opening was part of a flashback, a technique that can also be used with a biography told in chronological order. Instead of starting at the beginning, you start with whatever you feel is the most dramatic or interesting aspect of the person's life that can also stand alone. This should be an anecdote that, when taken out of context, is so interesting to read that you want to know more. Then you go from that to a transition that moves the reader to the beginning of the life. If the early years are critical but not all that interesting, starting in this manner can keep the reader involved instead of causing the person to set the work aside.

Once the opening has been established, the bulk of the text falls naturally into place. The subject's life sets the parameters for the book. There is a limited time frame. There are only so many areas of the world to be discussed.

The main problem will be how you write the material. What anecdotes do you have? What text is available to help you flesh out the material?

A biography should never be a recitation of facts. You are talking about the passions and pleasures of a person's life. This is an individual who has fallen in love, experienced sex for the first time, attempted to find a job, had moments of self-doubt and great triumphs. Your subject has faltered or been the victim of circumstances beyond his or her control. Every emotion we can experience in life has been experienced by your subject. To limit your writing to a statement that the person discovered the planet Pluto on August 12 belies the achievement. The biographer must show the subject's fascination with astronomy, the ceaseless study of the sky, the belief that there is something more in space than others know, and the ridicule the person may have borne for that belief.

Likewise it is important to understand the times and to recreate them. As I write this, newspapers and magazines are celebrating the 1960s with an emphasis on the Woodstock music festival. Nostalgia tells those who were there or wanted to be there that it was three days of good times, good feelings, and good music. There was love, peace, and harmony. The people who attended gave hope for a better world, a better life. They foretold an existence for which we are still striving. Or such is the myth.

The truth was that many positive interactions occurred. Several hundred thousand people managed to camp in a relatively small area without riots or extreme violence. But few truly interacted with the others. Drug use was rampant. Sex was a part of the celebration. Many of the participants were hedonists, out for a good time, to "get stoned, get laid, and hear some tunes," as one participant described it to me at the time. People tolerated the cramped conditions, often using LSD, marijuana, amphetamines, and other drugs to escape both the problems and real life.

Woodstock was a rock concert, the biggest that had ever occurred. It had nothing to do with crime on the streets, hunger, poverty, the curing of disease, or any other cause that might truly alter the human condition for the better. Some of the people who attended were drifters, one step up from street survivors. Others were serious music lovers who felt they wanted to be a part of so dramatic an event. And still others went to party in a way that had not been seen before or since. But it was still a rock concert and an accurate re-creation of those times must rely on what happened, not the myth that was created.

This is not to say that if the subject of your biography was changed by an event, the event was meaningless. It is important to show what happened historically as well as what was going on in the personal life of your subject.

For example, when I worked with Patricia S. Lawford in order to write the Lawford biography, one of his closest friends was Judy Garland who also died tragically because of substance abuse. He made notes stating, in effect, that they used to pal around together.

Peter's relationship with Judy was not all that important. The films they made together were never classics. Their lives, though interesting, were not so intertwined that I needed to explore what they did together. I could just mention the fact that they would pal around together and be done with it. Instead, whenever I talked with anyone who knew either one of them at the time they were friends, I asked about the relationship. I sought information concerning what they did together and how they did it. Then I filed it away without thinking about it until I was ready to write about that time period. When I again looked at the notes in my folder, I was amazed.

Judy Garland became a major Hollywood star because of the movie *The Wizard of Oz* that followed her roles in the string of successful movies she made with Mickey Rooney. Her rendition of "Somewhere Over the Rainbow" became a classic as well as a signature piece for her nightclub act. And Peter, though not well known, was earning excellent money. He was handsome, young, and successful. So naturally they went to all the best night spots, or so most people, myself included, would assume.

The truth was delightful, far more interesting than the fantasy.

Peter and Judy's idea of a date was to go bowling. The problem was that neither of them was any good. They bought bowling bags. They bought bowling shoes. Then they went out and played by their own rules.

Judy considered a gutter ball to be any ball that landed in some-one else's lane — and she got a lot of gutter balls. Peter had a crippled hand, his fingers sometimes locking in the ball so that he went part way down the alley, still holding his ball. They caused so much havoc that they were regularly banned from bowling alleys throughout southern California. And after each fiasco, they would buy carryout Chinese food to eat.

The story was delightful. It was an anecdote that said more about their character than the glitz, the glamour, and the drug addiction. It revealed an almost childlike, very human side to both of them.

Neil Baldwin's highly successful biography of photographer Man Ray (Emmanuel Radnitsky) used extensive anecdotes in order to reveal many facets of his character and those of the people around him. For example, there was a period of the 1920s when he fell in love with a woman who led an extremely Bohemian lifestyle in France. She was born to a woman so poor that the child was probably delivered on the streets. She grew to have great beauty and was a favorite model for artists of the day. She frequently dressed in oversized men's clothing and seemed to live on the street, some-times trading sex for a few nights' lodging with one of the artists. They would also buy her meals when she was starving, treating her like a sexy stray cat who neither claimed nor desired a master.

The model, who called herself Kiki of Montparnasse, was uneasy when she first posed for Man Ray because he was the first photographer with whom she had ever worked. Yet there was an instant attraction between the two of them, an attraction so intense that she lived with him for six years, taking the name Kiki Man Ray.

On page 107 of Baldwin's book *Man Ray American Artist* (Clarkson Potter, Inc., distributed by Crown Publishers; New York, 1988), Baldwin uses an anecdote to show the unusual relationship the two of them shared. He explains first how she was limited in her knowledge of makeup and dress, then states:

> They followed the same ritual every night before going out. After her obligatory hour-long bath, he designed Kiki's face and painted it on with his own hand. First Man Ray shaved her eyebrows completely, and then he applied others in their place, varying the color, thickness, and angle according to his mood. Her heavy eyelids, next, might be done in copper one day and royal blue another, or else in

silver or jade. A tiny cap with a brocaded veil, a beaded dress with a plunging neckline — a rose positioned strategically, to be removed at the height of the festivities and placed between her gleaming, perfect teeth — would complete the preparations, and they'd be ready, invariably accompanied by Kiki's steadfast companion Therese Teize. Therese and Kiki met during the three-day national holiday festivities during the summer of 1922, and Therese took a room near Kiki and Man Ray's in the Hotel Istria, at 29, rue Campagne-Premiere, next door to the studio. When Man Ray was off on fashion shootings out of town, Therese shared Kiki's bed.

The story continues, but look at what the anecdote adds to the period under discussion. Here is a woman who finds a man to whom she wishes to commit in ways she had never done before. At the same time, there is an obvious lesbian relationship taking place of which, to some degree, Man Ray has to be aware. In addition, we have a man who seems to treat the woman he loves like a doll, dressing her, applying makeup. It is an unusual situation at best and, in one paragraph, much is said about both of them during this rather unusual period in France.

Anecdotes not only make your book enjoyable to read, they also move the story in a way that keeps your reader turning the pages. They should be used as much as possible.

Quotes

There are several types of quotations that evolve when writing a biography. The first is the created quotation mentioned in chapter seven. Some children's book editors condone the use of created quotations in an effort to move the story. Other children's book editors feel that while a created quotation is interesting, it compromises the integrity of the biography. Their attitudes have much to do with the age range for which the writing is intended, of course. The younger the reader, the more likely the editor is to allow such a device. Check with the editor for the specific children's book you might be writing before creating such scenes. However, if you are writing for adults, a fake quotation must never be used. Except . . .

There are several concerns when quoting the words of the living and the dead. These include copyright restrictions that are far more strict than you might otherwise imagine. However, before getting into such restrictions, let's tackle the issue of what exactly is a quote.

Several years ago I had to interview a man for an article on real estate. He was a nationally known expert who knew that I was on a short deadline and respected that fact. I had only a half day in which to interview him, he had agreed to the interview, and he knew that if either one of us failed to keep the appointment, the deadline could not be met. Unfortunately we got together at the same time that his daughter had just had a baby, his first grand-child, and he had been up all night at the hospital. He was exhausted and his conversation left much to be desired.

The more the man talked, the more I realized that he was coming across as a confused fool. I understood what he was trying to say and the information was invaluable. I was receiving a tremendous lesson in real estate investment and I was most impressed with him. But the exact quotes would have made him look almost stupid when, in reality, he was simply exhausted from twenty-four hours with almost no sleep.

I had three choices for the article. I could quote his exact words, comfortable that the reader would gain essential information if he or she simply read between the lines. I could paraphrase what was said, giving the information without putting it into quotation form. And I could use quotes, changing what was said to what I knew my subject was trying to say. I chose the latter.

When I wrote the article I quoted the man as though I was using his exact words, yet I made changes such that they made sense when they hadn't before. I felt that I captured his phrasing and the way in which he talked (or the way in which he would have talked had he not been exhausted). I had a couple thousand article credits and several books when I met with him so I felt confident that I knew what I was doing. Then I turned the material in to the editor and did what any other writer would do under such circumstances. I held my breath.

The article appeared, the telephone rang, and my subject was on the telephone. "I just saw the article you wrote," he told me. "I have to tell you I was quite worried the day you interviewed me. I was exhausted from being up all night with my wife and daughter, and I was afraid that I wasn't making any sense. But you captured my words exactly. I wouldn't have changed anything had I seen it before it went to press. I'm delighted that I spoke so well and that you didn't change a word."

And then I exhaled.

Should I have put his words in quotation marks? Obviously I think that I did the right thing and my approach worked—that time. By contrast, John Brady, a professional writer and author of a book on interviewing that is considered a classic in the field, feels that you must never change a quote. A quote must be the exact words of the subject or it must be paraphrased, attributed to the source without the use of quotation marks. Anything else is both cheating and risking making a serious mistake.

What is the answer? I don't feel that there is one. I remain comfortable with slightly altering what is said when the exact words will be vague to the reader but the meaning is clear. Under no other circumstances will I change a quote. It is just too risky.

For example, there are many individuals in the public eye who are brilliant speakers. Former President Ronald Reagan was known as the "great communicator," a slight misnomer. Actually he was a brilliant speech reader, an actor who used his skills as president. A communicator is someone who conveys the full truth about an incident or event. Reagan was not one to make candid, off-the-cuff speeches to the public. He was skilled only with the written word, a situation with which he and his staff felt comfortable.

Other politicians are often similar to Reagan, as are many actors and others in the entertainment field. Some, like Reagan, are also good with an ad-lib.

There are writers who hero worship the individual they are interviewing. Perhaps they have seen them in a movie and mistake the character and the script for real life. Or they may have heard their subject give a speech that caused them to stand and applaud at the end. There could be any number of reasons. Whatever the case, they discover when they meet the individual that he or she is not particularly articulate or exciting. Even if the person is brilliant, there is a problem with communicating in an interesting manner.

This is especially true with entertainers. Jack Lemmon commented during an interview that there are no stupid, long-time stars on stage or in films. It takes intelligence to act with skill and survive over the years. However, the training for an actor does not always involve higher education. Actors may be high school dropouts or they may have attended college to participate in the acting classes, not to bother with the books. Some are self-taught. Many have limited intellectual backgrounds and sound a little like street thugs when they talk without a script. They are a disappointment compared with their on-screen persona.

A writer discovering that his or her hero has feet of clay is likely to want to cheat. The writer recognizes that the person is far brighter than he or she sounds and wants to "improve" the quotes. The phrasing might be changed. The person may become articulate. Foul language may be eliminated or minimized. And when the writer is finished, the information the subject imparted will be the same, but the way it was said will be quite different.

Is there anything wrong with cleaning up someone's speech if the message is still there? Many writers would applaud such an effort. However, a biography, and especially an as-told-to autobiography, at its best, is a part of history. We gain insights into the man or woman by what we read. Sometimes the language and phrasing can tell us far more than the words alone.

For example, Diane Sawyer's "ghosted" assistance with former President Richard Nixon's autobiography is intelligent, well reasoned, and interesting. Reading the book indicates that the man seems inherently decent, possibly incapable of most of the criminal actions attributed to him. This is fair and it is the view of history that he wants the reader to have. However, for future writers to rely on quotes from Nixon's book would mean to deny the public the true history of his administration.

A visit to the National Archives to arrange to listen to the tape recordings he secretly made during his term in office results in quite a different image of Richard Nixon. The language frequently spoken and recorded by Nixon and his associates is often quite foul. There is a sense of disdain not only for those who crossed his path in a manner he did not like, but seemingly for the American public as a whole. The language, quoted exactly, presents a much different picture of the president. And a transcription of some of the tapes, counterpointed with quotes from his "authorized" writings, reveals a very different man than would otherwise be known.

In instances where a change of quotes evolves from hero worship, such change should not be justified. You are creating a false impression that belies what should be a biographer's moral obligation to the truth.

Does this mean that Diane Sawyer should not have "cleaned up" the Nixon book if he used the same type of language in her presence? That is a quite different situation. The "ghosted" autobiography, and even the as-told-to, is meant to be the person's story as he or she wants it told. If that leaves a false impression, that false impression becomes fodder for the objective biographer to follow. In one instance, you, the writer, are telling the person's story as the subject wants it to be told. In the other, you are telling the person's story in a manner meant to be as accurate as possible. If the two should differ, so be it.

Who Owns Your Subject's Words?

There have been a number of changes in the copyright law over the years. Not only have writers gained more rights, so have individuals recorded by the electronic media.

Depending upon when they were written, the ownership of personal letters may not also include the copyright ownership. For example, suppose Famous Writer gives her letters to the Special Collections division of Undergraduate University's library. You want to write the unauthorized biography of Famous Writer so you go to Undergraduate University's library and there the head librarian brings you box after box of letters. These were all sent to the rich, the famous, and the not so famous. They talk of loves lost and won. They speak of heroism and bigotry. They reveal intimate details of everything from the way the writer thinks to the way she enjoys making love (immediately after consuming exactly eleven Toll House cookies and a glass of skim milk laced with one ounce of vodka while the strains of Vivaldi play on the stereo). And you say to yourself, "This is everything I need for the unauthorized biography. I'll supplement the work with interviews with friends, former lovers, editor, agent, and the like. But the state of her mind, the way she thinks and acts, they're all here. It's as much or more information as I would have obtained from an interview."

In fairness you request an interview with Famous Writer anyway and, as you suspect, she refuses to grant one. ("I'm a very private person. What I don't put into my books and shorter writing is no one's business. In fact, I'm not certain that even my books are anyone's business but I make too much money from them to stop right now.") In addition, when you ask the library director about quoting from the letters, the director states, "These are part of our collection. We have the complete ownership and can do with them as we wish. Yours will be the first complete biography to use the collection and, so long as you give us credit, we're delighted to have you quote anything you wish. Just give us an acknowledgment in the book."

But you are far more clever than anyone imagines. You not only get a photocopy of the agreement that gives the Undergraduate University Library full possession of the letters, you also get a statement, in writing, from the librarian, the president of the university, and the university lawyer saying that you may quote from the letters.

Now you set to work. You do your interviews. You read through the letters. You divide them by subject — early education, first romance, early writing efforts, relationship with editors, early criticism, work as a war correspondent and part-time waitress in Saigon, etc. You use them to weave a rich tapestry of words, some yours, others from the letters, until you have a wonderful book, a brilliant book, a book that sends thoughts of the National Book Awards dancing through your head. Your publisher schedules a

50,000-book first printing, ten times normal, a major book tour, advertising campaigns . . .

And your subject says, "No! You may not quote directly from my letters. I will gain an injunction to prevent you from using my work in that manner."

You expected this reaction, of course. You send your documents to Famous Writer's Big-Name Lawyer who looks at the agreements, pronounces them all in order, and laughs in your face. "Copyright!" shouts Big-Name Lawyer.

"End of book, author tour, awards, and lunch at Elaine's in Manhattan," says your publisher.

And you are looking dumbfounded.

Sound exaggerated? Not at all. When working with letters, ownership does not mean the transfer of copyright as a number of writers have discovered when developing unauthorized biographies of famous writers. The person receiving a letter, whether through the mail, as a gift (such as with archives or special collection), by purchase from a dealer in collectibles, or in any other manner, owns that letter. The writing itself is considered to still be within the copyright of the writer or his/her estate, depending upon when it was written and whether or not it was previously published. The exact circumstances should be checked by an attorney familiar with the copyright laws. However, the general rule is that if the person whose letters you wish to use is still living, there is a good chance that you will not be able to quote directly from the letters even when you have permission of the current owner. You may paraphrase the letters so long as the paraphrasing does not come too close to the original writing. You may write about their contents. But using the exact words or a paraphrasing very close to the exact words may require the permission of the original writer.

A similar situation exists with voices recorded after the copyright law went into effect in 1978. Should you interview someone on tape, you will need that person's permission to quote from the tape. This is not the case when the individual is making a public statement, such as a tape recording made at a press conference. But you will need permission to quote from your interviews, and you will need permission directly on the tape to be able to broadcast all or part of that interview.

The simplest way to handle this problem is to make certain the tape is recording, then say, "Let me check this with your voice level. I want to be certain the tape is recording what you are going to say so that I will be able to use it to quote you exactly when I am writing." The subject's acknowledgment is considered approval to quote. You might also start the interview, following this approach, with a statement such as, "The tape is working perfectly. I'll be able to get your exact words for the book."

Oddly, if you choose to just make notes or to make notes while you are taping, there is nothing wrong with quoting what is said based on your notes, even though your notes may be wrong. If your quotes seem to match your notes when checked by an impartial observer, they are acceptable. It would seem that the recording would be preferable, and it is, but there are some minor restrictions that do not exist for the handwritten words.

Fortunately I have yet to encounter someone who agreed to an interview with a tape recorder running who was not also comfortable with letting me quote him or her. However, I do not try to explain the copyright law to the person. I simply get permission to use the recorder, pull out my notebook for a backup, and start asking questions. In general, no one is going to talk with you in this manner unless they are also going to let you quote them.

A writer's published works are fair game for quoting. You will need permission from the publishing company should you wish to quote more than the number of words that constitute "fair use." This is a term that is rather vague. Some experts say that five hundred words or fewer constitute fair use when quoting from a book. This means that you may quote a maximum of five hundred words without permission. You must give full credit — the title of the book and the author (I usually add publisher and copyright date, though these are not necessary). But you need not get permission.

Other experts say that four hundred words is maximum. And some feel safe only when they don't exceed two hundred and fifty words. The important point is that quoting with attribution but without permission allows for minimal quoting. You also may not closely paraphrase longer passages to bypass gaining permission. Close paraphrasing is considered the same as quoting.

For example, suppose the passage you wish to quote reads:

> Sonia entered the room naked and dripping water from the shower, a towel wrapped about her waist, apparently oblivious to her condition as she sat at the typewriter we keep in the bedroom. Millicent was carefully positioned under the covers so it would look as though I was alone. Helga, under the bed, suppressed the need to sneeze from the dust that tickled her nostrils, Sonia always being too preoccupied with her writing to bother to dust our home. And Allison, hiding in the closet, was terrified that Sonia would discover her, then tell Allison's husband, Rex, with whom Sonia was having an affair she thought I did not know about.

Now we have a rather steamy passage about an unusual affair. One man, the "I" character in this kiss-and-tell memoir, apparently is involved with at least four women at once. It is uncertain whether three of the women enjoy his favors at the same time or if all four were naive about one another. Whatever the case, it shows the subject at his moral worst and you want to quote the passage.

Now suppose you have already used what your lawyer tells you is a "fair use" quote. And suppose the subject has informed you that he has just joined a Tibetan religious group and wants to put his old life behind him, never again discussing such affairs. This means a paraphrase or mention of the incident.

What is too close a paraphrase? Consider the following:

> In describing one rather bizarrc incident, he wrote of the time his wife, Sonia, entered the bedroom straight from the shower. She was still naked and had not bothered drying herself. Instead, she wrapped her waist with a towel, sat at a desk they kept in the bedroom, and began working at the typewriter.
>
> Meanwhile he was in bed with Millicent whom he had positioned under the covers in such a way that Sonia would not see her. He had also hidden two other women in the room—Helga was under the bed and Allison was in the closet. Allison was terrified of discovery because she knew her husband would learn she was unfaithful. He had been having an affair with Sonia that kept her too busy to dust her bedroom. As a result, Helga was constantly in danger of sneezing from the dust.

This was a paraphrase of the quote, but look how close it came to the original. The words are different yet the meaning is identical and all the information is provided. Such a paraphrase is probably in violation of copyright if permission is not received to use it.

A proper paraphrase, one that would not violate the Copyright Law, follows:

> In one rather outrageous story concerning his personal life, he described a night when he was engaged in sexual activity with three women while his wife, Sonia, was in the shower. She had an idea for a story that eventually became her best-selling novel, *Red Hot September* [Note: This was not in the original quote. It is additional information added as a result of further research and appropriate since the paraphrased story is not being quoted exactly]. She emerged quickly, just a towel around her waist, forcing him

> to get under the blankets, covering one woman with his
> body while the other two women hid under the bed and in
> the closet.

Notice how the pertinent information is provided, along with an extra detail that makes the story more complete within the context of his life. Not mentioned are the names of the women nor the details about the risk of sneezing or the additional love triangle. Those facts may come out elsewhere in the book or they may be omitted entirely. The importance of the quote is that it reveals two aspects of the subject's world—his self-centered personal life and the way in which his wife, a novelist, worked when inspired.

Now the original quote becomes just another piece of historic information in your writing. The source is noted in the bibliography, though the incident need not be annotated. Ideally the story will be supplemented through direct interviews or the personal writing of the women involved.

Don't Quote Me on That

There are times when your subject will tell you a story that you wish to use, yet you will be asked to not quote the person. Usually this comes when he or she is relaxed, says too much, then decides that it should be "off the record."

The truth is that nothing is "off the record" in most instances. There have been court cases related to newspapers where a confidential source, highly placed in a state or national government, provided a reporter with information on the condition that the person's name not be used. The quote was supposed to be attributed to an "anonymous source" or a "high-ranking White House official" or "an unimpeachable source" or a "government official" or whatever. Instead, the person's name was used, accidentally or deliberately. Sometimes the courts have ruled that the breach of trust was a shame but it was not improper. In other instances there have been court rulings that the agreement amounted to a verbal contract between the source and the writer. Publishing the name was a breach of that contract and the writer had to pay a penalty.

Yet in general the courts have held that the First Amendment of the Constitution gives a writer the permission to publish anything he or she obtains. There may be penalties for having the material. There may be penalties if the information is inaccurate and defames someone. But there is an inherent right to publish anything under the Constitution as written and interpreted.

There are several ways in which writers have tried to get around this issue. Sometimes they quote the individual but hide the person's identity. Sometimes they quote the individual by name. And sometimes they attempt to gain the same stories from others, figuring that if three or more people, ideally not friends of one another, tell the same story, it is accurate and no one will be able to trace the source.

The right and wrong of such situations is debatable. If the information is accurate and provable, if you have documented properly, you should use the statement. Sometimes it is important to deny the "off the record" request and name your source. At other times you will want to respect the confidence by saying something to the effect of "according to a close friend" or "according to a former employer/wife/lover/schoolmate/etc." And at still other times you will want to research the matter independently, get the same story from several sources, then not quote any one of them, telling the story as fact and knowing you can back it up later. There is no right way, none of the choices being wrong in a legal sense. You simply have to use your own instincts based on the circumstances as you view them.

Applying for Permission

Should you need permission to quote beyond fair use from published sources, the procedure is a simple one. Contact the "Rights and Permissions Department" of the publishing company involved. The publisher will be listed in the book. Some companies have a Rights and Permissions Department. Others do not. But with such an address, your request will get to the right person.

The address of the company can be found in any number of reference books. I usually start with the current *Writer's Market* published by Writer's Digest Books. If I do not find the address there, I contact the library where they check *Literary Market Place.* Generally the listing will be in one of these two. If not, the reference librarian will check further for me.

The letter is a simple one. I usually write something to the effect of:

"I am a professional writer who is currently writing a book on the life of [subject's name]. Toward this end I would like to quote the following passage(s) from [page number] of the book [title, author, date of publication]." Then I follow with the appropriate paragraph(s) so the publisher knows the exact section.

"Thank you for your time and trouble. I trust there will be no problem with gaining such permission." I also enclose a self-addressed, stamped envelope for the reply.

There may be a charge for such use. The credit line must be specific and you will have to ask what rights they receive. Also, there are instances where the publisher is not the rights holder and you must talk with the appropriate party (the author, author's estate, agent, or whomever).

A similar situation holds true with magazines and newspapers. Permission must be given for a quote. Toward this end I usually contact either the publisher or the managing editor of the publication. For magazine listings I start with *Writer's Market,* then check the library for *Ulrich's Guide to Periodical Literature.* Newspapers for everywhere in the United States are listed in the annual *Editor & Publisher Yearbook,* again a library reference volume.

Note: Should you live in a small community, there is a chance that your local library will not have a current edition of the volumes mentioned. You can call the reference section of the nearest big-city library for the information. Also, should your small town have a college or university, often the reference librarian for the school will be able to help you. Most schools set in smaller communities will provide such public services if a request is made.

Other Tricks of the Trade

The reading of novels is one way to improve your skills as a biographer. Novelists, unlike nonfiction writers, have to constantly be aware of the pacing of a story and what they are doing to make the reader keep turning the pages. This is not to say that a nonfiction writer can succeed with a boring book. No one reads a boring book unless they are compelled to do so for reasons that range from being in a class discussion about the volume to recognizing that the book is the only accessible source for essential information. Yet there are more people who will voluntarily read boring nonfiction than those who will read boring fiction. Editors recognize this fact and sometimes let their writers be more sloppy in presentation than they should.

Eventually such sloppiness hurts everyone. The publisher is reluctant to take another book by the writer unless, again, there are compelling reasons. Thus if someone is the only expert in a particularly needed subject, such as the treatment of a rare disease, he or she will be published. But given a choice, the number of works accepted by the editor will be limited.

Novelists lack such tolerance. They are creating a world in which no one has ever lived before. They are populating that world with people who have previously existed only in their imagination. And they are trying to convince the readers to spend a few hours' time sharing that world of their creation.

Ideally you have the integrity to make your biography the best possible book you can. You try to make the person about whom you are writing come alive through the anecdotes you relate, the description, and the other information you can impart. False dialogue is not used, but quotes may be juxtaposed so the text has the excitement of a story with dialogue.

Perhaps the greatest trick you can use with a biography is the novelist's method for keeping you turning the pages.

Have you ever had the experience of reading a book you cannot put down? You decide to read no more than a chapter before going to sleep, then find yourself still reading an hour or two later. And have you ever finished such a book, only to realize that the story really wasn't all that compelling? It wasn't the greatest book you have ever read. It wasn't the most exciting. There seems, on reflection, to be no reason why you should have reacted the way you did, yet you could not put down the book.

I am certain that this experience has happened to you as it has to me. In fact, after experiencing this reaction to several books, none of which were outstanding when I thought about them later, I began analyzing what made me feel compelled to turn the pages. That was when I discovered a trick that I have since used not only in my own fiction writing, but also in writing biographies. This is to let each chapter end with a high point unresolved at the start of the next chapter.

There are two ways novelists routinely end a chapter. The first is with everything neatly resolved, as though the chapter was a complete story unto itself. The second is with the chapter ending on a high point that is neatly resolved at the start of the next chapter. For example, look at the difference between two novels selected at random simply because I happen to be reading them at this moment. They are basic mystery and suspense fiction, each writer choosing one of the two approaches for chapter endings.

Jane Waterhouse, author of *Playing for Keeps* (Macmillan Publishing Company, New York, 1987), lets each chapter stand alone. The end of chapter 20 reads:

> The couple began to walk toward the battlements. Murtaugh stopped them with his voice.
>
> "What was the reaction of the others to this new part of the game?" he called softly.
>
> Katherine considered for a moment and then replied, "They thought it was funny at first, I guess. Like Eric and me. Then it started making everybody a little uncomfortable."
>
> "Except Jake and Rebecca," said Eric. "They really seemed to get off on it."

> Murtaugh wished them goodnight. He started down the hill by way of Castle Point, hearing the fireworks but never turning toward their brilliance.

There the chapter ends. You can set down the book or choose to continue. Chapter 21 can be read later, for it starts slowly:

> Tuesday was a working day, and for the first time in over two years David Rothman called in sick. To be sure, his throat felt a little scratchy, the signs of a cold—Janis had left out his sweaters when she packed for the mountains.

The chapter continues with other characters leading their lives. Each chapter is a complete, interrelated story moving toward the ending. I thoroughly enjoyed the book, yet I could read from chapter to chapter without feeling compelled to go on if there were other things to do.

The second approach, ending the chapter on a high point completed at the start of the next chapter, was used by coauthors Marilyn Cooley and James Edward Gunn for their book, *You'll Hear from Us* (St. Martin's Press, New York, 1989).

Chapter 2 has a police lieutenant who has not been directly involved with any sort of violence in the book leaving the home of his ex-wife. There was a scene introducing his relationship with her and their son. Then he drove toward home, stopping at a delicatessen to buy a turkey sandwich on white bread.

> He left the deli, eagerly anticipating dinner. The next second he was lying facedown on the sidewalk. A bullet had just roared past his ear and slammed into the brick building.

Who would not go on to chapter 3? And that chapter begins:

> A second bullet crashed into the plate glass window, shattering it. MacIver rolled toward the nearest cover, his station wagon, which was parked facing the curb. He had his Colt around the fender, he sighted the source of the shots, a Trans Am stopped on the street slightly ahead of and at right angles to his car. A third shot ricocheted off the curb beside him.

The action continues for two-and-a-half pages before it ends with the paragraph:

MacIver looked at the bullets and agreed that they were too damaged to be of any use in identifying the weapon they had come from. There wasn't much for him to do, so he headed home. As he drove, he wondered who the hell wanted him dead.

Then there is a visual space break and the story starts a new direction, much as Waterhouse's writing does at the start of each new chapter. Even though the writing is not so smooth in *You'll Hear from Us,* you have a tendency to read into the next chapter before stopping.

But there is a third approach to fiction regularly used by those writers whose work you can't seem to put down. It is this approach that can be adopted by the biographer most effectively.

Imagine a cliff-hanger ending typical of the old silent movies. The heroine, Hildegarde Wholesome, is securely tied and gagged, secreted in a locked closet inside an abandoned building that is about to be destroyed by a demolition company. Dynamite has been placed throughout the building, and it is being destroyed a section at a time by people who have no idea that she is trapped there.

The first section explodes, jarring her to consciousness. She twists. She turns. She tries desperately to free her hands and feet, only to discover that the ropes were expertly knotted. They not only hold, her struggles seem to cause them to tighten all the more. Then she screams, hoping that someone will hear her, but the gag muffles her voice enough that it does not carry past the closet.

The second explosion goes off, and this time dust falls on her. The wall shakes and Hildegarde realizes that the next blast may bring tons of brick and steel crashing down on top of her.

End of the chapter.

The reader decides to see how she gets out, if she does survive, and starts the next chapter. However, instead of staying at the demolition site, the story suddenly moves two thousand miles away. The new chapter begins with something along the lines of:

> Catherine Courageous was unaware of Hildegarde's plight as she climbed aboard Maxwell Manley's Lear Jet for their flight to Las Vegas. Suites had been booked, he told her. Champagne was on ice. And his credit line was hers to use. It would be a weekend filled with romance and excitement beyond her wildest dreams.

So what's happening to helpless Hildegarde? You read on,

reaching a point about two-thirds through the chapter where the jet starts to sputter and dip. Something is wrong with the fuel delivery system for, even though the gauges show plenty of gas in the plane, the pilot is having trouble keeping it in the air. They may have to jump or crash in the mountainous wilderness just outside of Nevada. "This is it," says Manley. "There's only one choice."

And now, with only two or three pages left in the chapter, we switch back to Hildegarde, either killing her off or freeing her from her predicament, depending upon the direction the plot needs to take. Then there is a quick switch back to the plane where Catherine is facing Manley who is wearing a parachute and holding a .45 caliber automatic to her head. He forces her to move away from the cabin door, announces that it was all a setup to kill her, and leaps from the sputtering plane. She stares in horror and we go to the next chapter.

It is Hildegarde's turn again, or perhaps Police Lieutenant Harry Heroic. Whatever the case, each cliff-hanger ending is not resolved immediately. You are drawn into a different but related story, taken to another cliff's edge, have your curiosity satisfied, then taken to yet another high point before changing directions. The cutting and pace are all logical, but because you cannot simply read from break to break as you would expect to do, you find yourself reading far more chapters than intended.

Biographies often have a similar, though usually less intense, potential. You can counterpoint several different stories in someone's career, bringing them together.

For example, let's take a look at one of the most frequently written biographical subjects, Abraham Lincoln. Everyone knows that he was shot by John Wilkes Booth at Ford's Theater. And it is dramatic to simply tell the story straight, letting the assassin enter the theater, go to Lincoln's box, and shoot him. It makes for an effective chapter and the next chapter can be the escape by Booth with the aid, sometimes unwitting, of others.

However, think of the ways that stories could be counterpointed based on the facts. You have the story of *Our American Cousin,* the British comedy playing at Ford's Theater. You can discuss the touring company, how they operated, and the attitude toward theater during Lincoln's day. You have the story of the assassination plot in general, the various participants, and what they hoped to gain. You have the story of Lincoln's relationship with his wife, always strained, as he weighs the decision whether to get away for the night. You have the story of the Pinkertons who were acting as bodyguards and a new security force in the nation. You have the story of Lincoln's premonition of death at some time in the future.

You have the story of John Wilkes Booth, himself. And you have the story of Dr. Mudd, the much maligned physician who would prove an unwitting aid in the escape. By interweaving all of these elements, you have a highly dramatic and unusual series of chapters that can be made every bit as compelling as the novel you cannot put down, even though the outcome is known to most readers.

Certainly not all lives have such drama throughout. But there are enough points in every subject's life where you can counterpoint what is happening in order to keep the reader's attention riveted to the page. Just in the way the story is told, you give the reader a book that he or she cannot put down.

Concluding the Book

Ending a biography is a fairly simple matter since only one of three situations may exist. The simplest is that the person is dead. If the subject has been dead for several years to several centuries, a certain amount of historic perspective is possible. Someone who has just died is less easy to handle because the full impact of the individual's life and work may not be understandable.

The second situation is that the person is alive but extremely elderly. The book is the subject's "last hurrah." The subject is reflecting back on a life that is essentially complete.

And the third is the person who is younger, perhaps midcareer such as Patty Duke was when she wrote *Call Me Anna*. There are many productive years ahead, years that may take the individual into an entirely different area.

If the person is elderly, the ending is usually one of personal reflection. There may be a poignant, humorous, or rather ironic comment summing up the entire story. It is simple and without problems.

The person who is in the middle of life, with many more stories to tell, is in a different situation. The ending needs to reflect the tone of the book without creating a situation that could prove embarrassing for the subject in the years ahead.

For example, when I wrote *DeLorean* with car magnate John DeLorean, he had triumphed over one court case but was facing more litigation. His wife had left him for a lover she had had during the last three years of their marriage. His daughter was partially in his custody, partially with his ex-wife. The facts in the cases were such that it was obvious he would ultimately triumph, a belief that has since come to pass in the various court appearances. But he was battered, without adequate funds, and in a bad situation. This was not a book where I wanted to write an upbeat ending. Instead,

I chose to tell a story that John had told me as we worked.

John had taken his daughter, Kathryn, to dinner. Composer Nelson Riddle was also in the restaurant, having dinner with Mrs. Meredith Wilson, the wife of the composer of "The Music Man." They were watching the animated conversation between John and Kathryn during their "night on the town," Kathryn having to return to her mother's custody the next day. I told the story of Riddle coming to their table.

" 'I never saw two people have a more wonderful and loving time,' he said. 'I have four daughters, and I envy you.'

"Somehow, I don't think he would have envied me the next evening when my daughter called me in tears.

"Apparently Kathryn had been thinking all day about our fun evening together, about the fact that her parents now lived apart, that her mother had married another man, and that her young, secure world had been shattered.

" 'What's wrong, honey? Why are you crying?'

" 'Oh, Daddy, I had to talk to you. I'm so sad. I saw a commercial on TV that made me cry. It showed a daddy and his little girl holding hands, walking in the woods. The leaves were changing color, just like when you and I used to walk in the woods and pick flowers.

" 'It reminded me of when we were happy.' " (From *DeLorean* by John Z. DeLorean with Ted Schwarz; Zondervan Publishing House; Grand Rapids, Michigan; 1985)

The ending is sad. It is not self-serving. It does not demand pity or compassion. It is a reality with which he had to live and it did not talk of grandiose schemes for the future, revenge, or anything else.

Perhaps the most obvious problems that can arise with someone who is living and makes grandiose statements about the future occur when life changes. Leading television evangelists are found to have had affairs and to misuse money. Athletes who were once role models for children are caught with drugs or embarrassed because they are selling their autographs to young fans. The perfect marriage "forever" ends in divorce (Christina Ferrare, John DeLorean's wife, published a book, *Style,* in which she glorified a marriage that was already a sham). Thus you want to end the book simply, effectively based on the story, without making a statement that you or your subject will live to regret.

By contrast, Don Graham's biography of Audie Murphy, the most decorated soldier of World War II, ended with the type of evaluation of Murphy's life allowed as hindsight after a death. He wrote:

Audie Murphy's was not the kind of life that Americans like to emulate. It lacked the Iacocca curve, the continuously upward spiral toward the dizzying heights of great wealth, great power. From age twenty-one on, Audie Murphy's life was a postscript to battle; the success he enjoyed ten years later, in 1955, was actually the beginning of a long, slow decline that came only after much pain, much struggle, and a descent into the labyrinthine depths of America in the 1960s. In the end, at the personal level, Audie belongs with Elvis Presley, whom women thought he resembled in his nocturnal paranoia. Audie, Elvis, and Hughes were all representatives of American dreams gone astray.

Maybe they were right, those friends of Audie's who thought he belonged in an earlier age, on the frontier, patrolling the streets of some flyblown Western town, keeping the peace. But he didn't live then; he lived in a time of change when the idea of heroism was itself open to challenge on every front.

Audie Murphy, impoverished child of agrarian America, trained executioner, champ solider of World War II, B+ cowpoke, husband, father, lover of uncounted women, poet, songwriter, compulsive gambler, friend of pugilists, grafters, jockeys, Mafiosi, and congressmen— what an extraordinary life he lived. On the edge, the way the Kid from Texas, the Quiet American, always preferred it.

— Quote from *No Name on the Bullet: A Biography of Audie Murphy* by Don Graham (Viking, New York, 1989).

The important point is that within the parameter of facts it is necessary to tell your subject's story in as interesting and entertaining a manner as possible. You can use all of the tricks of the novelist's trade except the creation of dialogue, false history, or other fictions. You make your subject come alive and your readers will eagerly await your next book, and your next.

TEN

How to Market Your Biography

W ho is your publisher? It is a question I am regularly asked at writers' conferences and by individuals just starting out in this field. It is presumed that publishers tend to produce one type of book and that all approach the same markets in the same manner. In fact, most people are quite surprised when I say that the publisher depends upon the book I have written. There is no one publisher I use because there is no one publisher who is right for each category of book. If you take a dozen publishers who claim they want biographies, you may find that some only want biographies for children, others want biographies of twentieth-century women or sports figures or entertainers. Each has found a particular marketing niche and they often do not want to publish in any other field. More important for you, the marketing department may not be able to handle the placement of other types of biographies.

Do I Need an Agent?

There is more nonsense written about agents than any other subject in the field of writing. Agents are generally the hottest topic of conversation among beginning writers. With an agent, all things are possible. Agents open doors, sell your book, make you rich, famous, and successful. Agents walk on water and, if they ever die, have their own private entrance to heaven. Agents are mythological beings who sit atop Mt. Manhattan and control the destiny of anyone who dares to take pencil/pen/typewriter/word processor in hand.

Without an agent, your writing will never sell. Without an agent, the sun will not rise in the morning. Without an agent, the world as we know it would cease to exist. Without an agent ... Well, you probably get the picture. I'm being facetious or sacrilegious, depending upon your viewpoint.

Please, don't get me wrong. I like agents. They serve a useful purpose in their place, just like automobiles, jetliners, and passenger trains. It's just that they are not the omnipotent, omniscient beings writers fantasize them to be. More important, if this is your first book, they don't want you, you don't want them, and, glory hallelujah, the publishers would rather not be bothered.

The Good Agent

I often joke that a good agent is one who loves and successfully represents my work while a bad agent does not. This is a variation of my belief that a good editor buys my work and a bad editor rejects it. (I realize that my list of bad editors may be your list of good ones, but that is a philosophical matter I'd rather not discuss here.) In all seriousness, though, there are some ways to find a good agent.

First, a good agent works in Manhattan and lives close enough to the city that he or she can be walking the streets every day. I am referring, of course, to book agents. Agents handling film projects should work in the Hollywood area, living near there. But the skills and the businesses are so radically different that a great Hollywood film agent is, at best, a weak book agent. Likewise, a book agent has no business representing you to Hollywood unless he or she has an associate in the Los Angeles area who does nothing but handle projects there.

Great agents are highly unlikely to live in Michigan, Florida, Washington state, Arizona, Illinois, or any other state outside of the two major market areas. The rare agent who lives in such an area has to be brilliant to be adequate because the commute is just too great to keep up with the marketplace. This is because an agent who is of any real value to you is daily able to knock on the doors of the publishing companies, meeting with editors, learning what they are buying today and where they are heading in six months to two years. There are handfuls of publishers in many cities throughout the United States. There are literally hundreds of book publishers in New York City. Any agent who is outside the mainstream, no matter how well intentioned, may not be able to represent you with the effectiveness of one who is daily in the mainstream of the American publishing world.

The agent should be a member of the Independent Literary Agents Association (ILAA, 15th Floor, 55 Fifth Avenue, New

York, New York 10003) and/or the Society of Author's Representatives, Inc. (SAR, Box 650, Old Chelsea Station, New York, New York 10013). The ILAA is a national group while the SAR concentrates on New York agencies. Both have ongoing training programs for agents as well as a code of ethics. It is possible that a member may not be good, but it is harder to find a good agent who is not a member than a bad agent who is a member. Just for your awareness, Hollywood agents or agents selling to film and television should belong to Writers Guild of America, East or West. WGA, West is located at 8955 Beverly Blvd., Los Angeles, California 90048. WGA, East is located at 555 West 57th Street, New York, New York 10019.

A good agent may or may not charge a reading fee, but the agent's income should be based on a percentage of sales. This is usually 10 percent of everything earned from the project the agent is handling for you, though some agencies now charge 15 percent. Any charge greater than 15 percent is considered improper in this business.

I am personally hostile to reading fees because I have known agents who make the bulk of their money from such charges. However, there is a logic behind the fees.

First, this is the writer's first book (if you have at least one published book put out by a legitimate national publisher, there should be no reading fee—you have proven yourself). Unless there is something special about it, the advance will be quite low, perhaps $5,000 to $7,500 if you are lucky. The money will be paid in increments, either half on signing and half on delivery, a third on signing, a third upon completion of half the manuscript, and a third upon delivery, or in some other manner. Whatever the case, the agent's commission is likely to be $500 to $750 total. For this, the agent has had to read each draft of your manuscript as it comes in, analyze the market, contact appropriate editors, submit the book, talk on the telephone, and meet the overhead of an office in one of America's most expensive cities. The agent will be lucky to clear minimum wage for the time involved.

Certainly the book may become a major best seller. The agent who turned down $1,500 (10 percent commission) for the Lawford book would ultimately have reaped more than ten times that amount for handling the project, and I am an established author whose books frequently sell better than average. However, it is equally likely that the book will not earn back the advance. In that case, though no money is ever returned to the publisher, the publisher will also not be paying you anything more. And, frankly, most first books do not earn back the advance before going out of print.

In addition, the first draft (and sometimes the final draft) of a first-time biography is likely to be terrible. It cannot be instantly sold and the agent has to risk so offending the ego of the writer that the writer may decide to sell it some other way. Thus the reading time may be wasted, lost income for the agent.

The reading fee, in the minds of those who charge them legitimately, forces the writer to be serious and pays for time that could otherwise have been spent servicing existing clients. A writer who pays a fee is also more likely to listen to suggested changes than may be necessary to ensure a sale.

Before paying the fee, you have the right to certain information. Most important, what is the ratio of income from reading fees to income from sales of manuscripts? The percentage income from reading fees should be very low or you may have a problem.

Is the reading fee returned after a sale is made? Is the reading fee charged against the agent's regular commission? Or is the reading fee kept in addition to the agent's commission after sale? Most agents charge the reading fee against the commission they will earn after the sale of your book so you only are out money if the book does not sell. Otherwise that fee is a part of what you would have paid in any case.

You should also ask if there are any other fees. Some agents charge for photocopying manuscripts or ask the writer to supply additional photocopied manuscripts for marketing. They may also charge for postage and long-distance telephone calls. Such fees are valid, though most agents in my experience are not currently billing their clients in this manner.

A good agent is *not* a writing teacher. You are not going to get line-by-line or page-by-page criticism. You will be expected to provide the best manuscript of which you are capable and not look to the agent to restructure it. If it is competent when submitted, it is probably marketable. If it is not, the agent should point up general problem areas that need correcting, if you are paying a fee. However, if it is really terrible, expect a polite form rejection, usually saying that the schedule is such that he or she does not see how you can be taken on as a client at this time.

The good agent will be more enthusiastic if this is your first biography but one of several books you have published. The agent will be even happier if you have more than one biography to your credit. Should this be your first book, the good agent may wish to have you complete the book, whatever that may mean, before representing you. This is because most new authors never finish their projects, even when under contract. This is shocking but true. It is easier to research and start a book, then talk about it endlessly to friends, co-workers, and casual acquaintances than it is to actually finish it. Most first-time authors do not finish what they start, even when under contract (a reason some publishers pay no advance until the book is completed).

Finally, a good agent will be capable of handling all sales related to your book or have contacts with people who can supplement their efforts. This means such subrights as magazine excerpts, newspaper syndication, paperback sales, and similar markets where appropriate, not to mention using others for overseas sales and Hollywood.

The Bad Agent

The bad agent makes money on reading fees. He or she probably does not live in New York or its environs, making periodic trips to Manhattan to meet with publishing personnel. In some cases, the agent just mails the work, handling matters the same way as you can yourself.

The bad agent has no track record to speak of. In addition, the bad agent's sales have probably been limited to those publishers where he or she has friends. The bad agent does not explore new markets, nor does the person keep up with changes within the various publishing houses.

The bad agent may be sincere but naive. For example, one bad agent in Arizona knows only the small "literary" houses where a "big" advance might only be four hundred or five hundred dollars. She made sales for her clients, never having the skills to learn if larger houses with better distribution might have offered more money. The publishers had limited methods for getting the books into the stores and the books, though bound, died sooner than might have been necessary based on their quality.

The bad agent considers his or her client list a closely guarded secret. He or she may feel that you are being blessed with the agent's skill instead of recognizing that, without your work, the agent would be unable to make money.

The bad agent is lacking in awareness of subrights potential. He or she may come to you for suggestions concerning where to sell the material after it is in book form. You may be asked about paperback houses, magazines interested in excerpts, and Hollywood contacts. Yet the purpose of the agent is to alleviate these concerns.

The Agent's Value to the First-Time Author

If you can get a good agent, there are only three areas of value for you. The first is the fact that book editors often read agented manuscripts before reading anything else. This is because they assume that the material sent is appropriate for their needs. They assume that the agent knows that the book is typical of what the publisher has been selling in recent years and plans to offer as part of its future lists. They also assume that the book is readable, something many unagented submissions are not.

Second, the agent saves your having to learn the publishing business well enough to sell your own book. However, I feel that every author should understand the business, the reason why this chapter will tell you how to sell your book without an agent's assistance. Unfortunately the learning process is ongoing so, without an agent, you will still have to keep aware of what takes place in the industry.

Third, the agent knows how much money to request and how to structure your contract. Some publishers try to keep all the money they can get. Other publishers give the best contract they can the first time out. Still other publishers like to negotiate even though their contracts read as though they have been etched in stone. Fortunately the Authors Guild, Inc. (234 West 44th Street, New York, New York 10036) has a sample contract it will send you for a nominal fee. This will show you how to read and understand what you have been sent. In addition, once you have a contract in hand, almost any agent will negotiate for you because there is no longer time needed to read your book or handle any other tasks. A percentage of even the lowest advance will easily cover his or her time when the only remaining task is negotiating percentages.

But What About the Publishers' Attitudes?

Almost no book editor will refuse to look at unagented manuscripts. Many dislike working with agents as a general rule because it is easier to handle everything directly with the author, the person with whom they will be producing the book. Occasionally a company announces that it will only take books submitted by agents, but this is a rarity in the business.

The confusion for many writers comes when a publisher announces that the company will not look at "unsolicited manuscripts." Many first-time authors mistakenly assume that "unsolicited" means unagented. It does not.

To make your manuscript "solicited," all you have to do is make contact with an editor who agrees to read it. Then the manuscript is sent, addressed to the specific editor, perhaps with the words "Requested Manuscript Enclosed" printed on the envelope. (How you make contact with an editor will be discussed later in this chapter.) This process reduces the workload of the editorial staff and assures that the topic seems appropriate. There is no guarantee of purchase. The book may be found unsuitable or even badly written. But it is "solicited" and will get read.

I have had many senior editors tell me that though they seldom find salable books coming in "over the transom," they read everything in their slush piles. "Any editor who doesn't read everything that comes in is a fool," one editor commented, and her statements were echoed by many others. "People die. I can't say it more bluntly than that. Tommy Thompson was one of my writers. He developed cancer and was dead thirty or forty years earlier than he should have been. People change professions. When was the last time Alex Haley wrote a book like *Roots* or *The Autobiography of Malcolm X*? He's done some things, but basically he's out of the business and into television work.

"I'm as hostile to someone whose submission screams 'beginner' as anyone else. I don't want to see green ink and script type. I don't want someone being cute, lightly gluing pages together at random to see if I really read the book. But if the manuscript is presented properly and the book reads well, I don't care if the writer's done nothing professionally. If I like it, if it fits our list, I'll offer a contract.

"Agents screen what they send most of the time. And when I'm pressured, I'll read something the agent submitted first. I'll even read more of a bad book if an agent submitted it than I will if it's in the slush pile because I figure the agent must have seen something to make him send it to me. But a bad book's a bad book and a good book's going into the marketplace, and I don't care how it gets to me. It's what's on the paper that matters."

It's what's on the paper that matters. There are no shortcuts, including agents. Good work sells. Bad work doesn't. The agent is not critical to the process. Your work is.

Who Buys Biographies?

Should you decide to sell your book yourself, as so many others do, your first concern comes with identifying the publishers who are interested in biographies and as-told-to autobiographies. Most writers think that if they simply send their book to a "big name" such as Random House or Doubleday, it will be published if the book is any good. Unfortunately, such reasoning is fallacious.

There are three sources for the information on publishers seeking biographies available to you. The first, and least effective, is to use such reference works as *Books in Print* and *Forthcoming Books in Print*. While these are excellent resources for many things, I find them more trouble than they are worth at this stage in your research.

The second source is any large, new bookstore. Check the biography section as well as specialized areas where such books may be kept. These include History, Social Studies, Contemporary Affairs (the exact terms used will vary with the store or the chain), Psychology, Music, Theater, Film, and New Books. The books may be shelved as Biography or placed on the shelf related to the field in which your subject excelled. Look to see the types of books being offered and the names of the publishers as listed just inside the volumes.

The third source is the one I find best. This is the magazine *Publishers Weekly*, which in February and August of each year produces issues that look like small-town telephone books. The bulk of these issues is devoted to advertising by the majority of book publishers in the United States. They present their Spring-Summer (February issue) and Fall-Winter (August issue) lists. The specific week that the special issues are released will vary each year but your library will have the back copies. There are also two special issues for children's books and religious books, each with different companies advertising than those advertising in the Spring and Fall Announcements issues.

Not all publishers appear in the special issues. Some like to advertise a week or two before or after the big ads in the hope that they will make greater impact in the marketplace. But you will have hundreds to choose from, all of them listing their complete line of forthcoming books.

Go through the advertising and see who publishes biographies and as-told-to autobiographies. Also note which publishers produce books in the fields where your biography relates. For example, a publisher of science books might be interested in the biography of a scientist whose work specifically relates to the publishing house specialty (e.g., a biography of Steve Jobs or An Wang, both computer geniuses, might be purchased by a publisher of computer books who would otherwise not consider a biography).

Next contact the appropriate publishers concerning your book. Ideally you will contact the appropriate editor who has handled other biographies. This is a task that may seem impossible at first, especially with those companies that claim they never give out editors' names. However, there are some tricks of the trade that will work.

Locating Specific Editors

The majority of publishing companies will give you the names of their editors or the appropriate contact person for querying about a biography. Call the company (the annual *Writer's Market* lists many telephone numbers, as does *Literary Market Place*). If all else fails, call information for the city where the publisher is located. Ask for the editorial department and request the name of the appropriate editor for querying about a biography or as-told-to autobiography. Most of the time the name will be provided or you will be given the name of the assistant.

In rare instances, the publishing company will not provide the name. "We like to keep our editors confidential," is the statement made, though the reasons are usually not very important. Sometimes writers inundate the editors with telephone calls and they genuinely cannot get their work done. At other times the publishing companies simply have a policy that the editors do not regard as necessary. The editors will gladly talk, those speaking before writers' groups freely giving out their office numbers, always making themselves available for new writers.

What happens when you cannot get an editor's name by calling? There are several approaches. The best involve checking both *Writer's Market* and *Literary Market Place* for names. Many times they are listed, along with their specialty in-house, even when the publishing company operator or editorial department receptionist will not give them out.

At other times you cheat.

Yes, cheat. I'll be honest. If the only way I am going to be able to get my material before the appropriate editor is to lie, then I will do so. My books cannot speak for themselves if no one has a chance to read my proposals. Thus I will do whatever is necessary to get the name of the right person to whom I must send the book proposal.

The following are approaches I have used, along with approaches others have used. Several of the writers who taught me these methods earn $100,000 or more in a bad year. Yet all of us share the same problem. We are only as good as our next book and often the person with whom we are speaking is not impressed with our past. Everything but trickery and deceit have failed after we went through the market listings we knew about and made the decision to not use an agent. In no particular order, try any or all of the following:

1. Call the publicity department and ask for the name of the editor who handles biographies. If you are asked why, explain

that you are writing an article for your local newspaper's book review section and need some quotes from editors making the decisions concerning what books to buy, how they'll be handled, and so forth. You won't need more than five or ten minutes' time, and you're contacting several houses. Almost invariably you will get the name you are seeking. Sometimes the publicist will want to set up the interview, in which case I evade slightly, explaining I am still working out my time schedule. In addition, there is the bonus that sometimes I really can sell such an article, conducting the interview and gaining even more information than I would otherwise have obtained.

2. Tell the operator that you are embarrassed. Your spouse met an editor at a recent party, talked about your book, and the the editor suggested sending a proposal. Your spouse wrote down the name on a piece of paper that you accidentally trashed. You've just typed out the material and want to send it but can't reach your husband/wife and have no idea who the appropriate person is. Who handles such things? And if there is more than one editor, have the operator give you two or three names that you can run by your spouse when he or she calls from his or her hotel room that night. (If this does not work, try at a different hour. Usually the operator you reach first thing during the day will go to lunch by 12:30 and a relief will take over. Listen to the voice and call back until someone else answers, then ask the same thing. Generally either the regular operator or the relief operator will be helpful.)

3. Use the approach for number 2 with the receptionist for editorial (just ask for the editorial department). If the company has a message desk, the person manning such a desk may be able to help.

Presenting Your Material

The first part of your book presentation is the proposal. This can begin in any number of ways. Often it is identical to what will be the opening of your book. At other times the writing is more general, setting the scene for what you plan to discuss. In every case it is most like an article written about a book, an article that discusses the beginning, middle, and end of what you will be writing in much longer form if the book is accepted.

For example, the following is the opening for a proposal I wrote in order to sell a book on the artist Ernest Blumenschein.

It is hard to imagine a more unlikely beginning for a major American art movement of the early twentieth century. Ernest Blumenschein was a dude, a dandy, a would-be cowboy whose fantasies were not enough to stop him from playing tennis, bridge, and dressing formally for dinner in the midst of some of the roughest wilderness land in America. Fred Harvey was a restaurateur, a British gentleman whose goal in life was to bring a fine dining experience to men and women crossing the United States on the previously uncivilized Atchison, Topeka, and Santa Fe Railroad. And finally there was L'Académie Julian, once considered the most disreputable art school in all of Paris and an unlikely catalyst for the last men and women who would devote themselves to capturing the dying American West on canvas and in sculpture.

L'Académie Julian

M. Julian was a Parisian hustler. He would do anything and everything for money. He boxed professionally, then posed as a model when younger men of greater speed and skill began beating him in prize fights. Finally he was almost penniless, having just enough money to rent a studio for a few weeks. He had no trade, no skill, but he did know the love affair nineteenth-century artists held for Paris. He also knew from his days as a model that many would pay anything, go anywhere, if they thought they could gain greater knowledge of painting. That was when the idea of opening his own school became, to him, a logical one.

Using showmanship that was only slightly more sophisticated than more modern matchbook advertising, he placed a sign reading "Academie de Peinture" outside his studio. For days he sat alone, unable to afford any greater promotion, yet unable to draw even one student to his headquarters. Then, as he faced almost certain bankruptcy, one youth slowly trudged up the stairs to see what courses were offered. Before he could escape, Julian grabbed an easel, pushed it in front of the student, and mounted the posing stand. Then, as the naive youth decided to stay and paint, "l'Académie Julian était fondée." Or so Julian bragged after his school grew to relatively massive quarters in the rue du Fauboug St. Denis where separate facilities for men and women existed.

The reason for that opening was because I wanted to sell a different type of art book. I wanted to show the editor that the book would not only discuss the artists and their work, but it would also provide both a historical perspective and be fun to read. The book was being sold for the general reader, not just the scholarly art buff, and the opening had to make that point to the editor.

A different approach was used with the proposal for my biography of Folke Bernadotte, a hero in Swedish history who is relatively unknown in the United States. Bernadotte was a man who seemed most aptly described by the British colloquialism "twit" during his early years. He was related to the king of Sweden but seemed to lack both direction and intellect. His family was extremely important in both politics and society, but he was content playing soldier in military units that were not expected to see action, working as a bank clerk, and generally marking time through life. The high point of his work was with the Boy Scouts until he became head of the Swedish Red Cross toward the end of World War II. He also became aware of the rescue work being done on behalf of French women in concentration camps, something that intrigued him as well.

Ultimately, through a series of unusual events, Bernadotte saved more than thirty thousand men, women, and children from the concentration camps of Nazi Germany. Some were Scandinavian, others Polish, French, and other nationalities. There were Christians and Jews, including people who emigrated to Israel and joined the Stern Gang that was fighting to free Palestine from British control. And it was the Stern Gang of terrorists, led by men who went on to the highest personal power in Israel, who murdered Bernadotte in Israel in 1948.

The book had to counterpoint several lives to tell Bernadotte's story. He was the pivotal character, of course. But other essential individuals included the creator of the death camps, Heinrich Himmler, who had to turn against Hitler in order to help Bernadotte, and Walter Schellenberg, Germany's top spy, who used both men as a means of avoiding execution for his work during World War II.

The story is both fascinating and quite complex. Yet in order to sell the book, I needed to find a way to show the editor what I intended to write. The successful proposal began as follows:

Walking with the Damned: The Folke Bernadotte Mission is the never-before-told story of one of the most dramatic periods of World War II. It is the story of a mission that eventually freed more than thirty thousand people, approximately half of whom were Jews, from concentration camps where they would have otherwise been murdered. It is also the story of several men, each driven toward different ends by the same means.

First there was Count Folke Bernadotte, the unlikely organizer of the dramatic rescue. He was a member of the Swedish royal family whose relatively undistinguished life gave no hint of the courage and dedication he would eventually reveal. He was married to great wealth, served in the military, yet never achieved more than a leadership position in the international Boy Scout movement. He had known the sorrow of losing two sons and the underlying fear of being a hemophiliac, a man for whom even minor injuries could provoke uncontrollable bleeding. Yet the idea that such a man would eventually be responsible for saving thousands of lives seemed extraordinarily unlikely.

Next there was Heinrich Himmler, Hitler's toady and the man who designed the death camps. By the time he met with Bernadotte, his madness led him to the belief that he would take control of the Third Reich, bringing Germany through the postwar years when Hitler no longer would be alive. Bernadotte was able to play on Himmler's delusion in a manner that caused the SS leader to violate Hitler's orders and cooperate in what should have been an impossible mission.

Walter Schellenberg, Germany's master spy, was more astute than Himmler, recognizing that all was lost for Germany and that the leaders who were not killed would go to jail. For him, the Bernadotte mission was a way to stay alive. It was better, in his mind, to save thirty thousand people "deserving" of death than to be put to death himself. To Schellenberg, the Bernadotte mission seemed a way to assure himself of the protection of Swedish asylum.

And Dr. Felix Kersten, who became Himmler's personal physician to avoid being sent to a concentration camp, developed a method for influencing the SS leader when he was at his weakest. His efforts behind the scenes tainted him as a Nazi yet helped assure the success of the Bernadotte mission.

Finally there are the other two stories that are interwoven, the Jews and other prisoners of concentration camps such as Ravensbruck, Neuengamme, and Theresienstadt, as well as the Stern Gang of Palestine. The latter eventually assassinated Bernadotte, though not before some of the Jews he had saved joined the ranks of the anti-British, terrorist organization.

The combined story is one of the most dramatic to come from World War II, as fascinating as an action/adventure novel, yet all of it true. The Bernadotte mission had one of the most unusual casts of characters ever to emerge in recent history.

The Bernadotte mission mentioned in the proposal related to his effort to win the release of concentration camp prisoners. The story was so complex that the full proposal ran approximately fifty pages in length, two to three times the length I normally need to sell a book.

Proposal Do's and Don'ts

The biggest difference between a proposal that sells and one that is likely to be rejected is the way in which you try to promote your book. The editor wants to see only three things in the proposal. The first is what the book will be about. The second is the writing style. And the third is an explanation of who will be interested in reading the book. Let us look at each of these issues separately.

1. What is the book about? This question is answered by giving the background on the subject of the biography. Ideally you will show that the life is fascinating for the casual reader. This should be someone who is either famous (or infamous), whether because of historic actions, personal achievement in the arts, politics, business, etc., or has led a fascinating existence. Side issues to be covered in the book, such as a period of history and your approach to telling the story, should also be explained.

For example, in the Bernadotte proposal I explained that I was going to counterpoint the story of Bernadotte's mission to save the prisoners with the behind-the-scenes plotting of top Nazis and the story of the Stern Gang. I showed how all three elements would ultimately come together when Bernadotte was assassinated, broadening the appeal of the book.

When I sold the Lawford biography, I showed how the book would reveal the behind-the-scenes story of the Hollywood star factory of the 1940s. It would show the private life of the Kennedy family, Peter's first in-laws. And it would discuss the drug and alcohol abuse that affected Peter and so many other Hollywood lives. The book would thus be a story on several levels, each having the potential to draw readers with special interests.

2. Showing the writing style. This is not something you can create. Style is simply the way you write. There is no right or wrong approach except when using incorrect English. Does your presentation seem to show that the book will be fun to read? Does it seem to be accurate and thoroughly researched?

Do you seem to write well enough so your reader will keep turning the pages? These are all questions the editor will want to mentally answer as he or she reads your book.

3. Who will be interested in your book? This question is harder to answer. Most beginners simply say, "Why, everyone will be interested in my book." Yet we all know from our own experiences that we tend to gravitate toward certain types of books and not others. Perhaps if we actually read some of the others we would be interested in them. But unless someone shows us how interesting a book might be, we usually don't take the trouble to find out. Thus it is necessary to pinpoint the predictable market.

For example, the Peter Lawford book had definite appeal to people interested in the history of the film industry, an identifiable group with their own book club. It also would appeal to history buffs since Peter was the brother-in-law of President Jack Kennedy and was a close friend until Kennedy's murder. In addition, there was an appeal for Kennedy buffs, a group that is separate from those interested in the history of American politics. Finally there were the big names who were a part of Peter's story—Marilyn Monroe, Judy Garland, Nancy Davis Reagan, and numerous others. Each of these aspects of the book had an identifiable market.

The Bernadotte book was not so simple. There are the people interested in the Holocaust and World War II in general, again both identifiable by publishers with past sales to readers interested in the same subject. Less predictable are those interested in the history of Israel during the revolt against British rule and the international market. However, I learned that an autobiography of Bernadotte published immediately after the war sold one hundred thousand copies in Sweden alone. This indicates an intense historical interest and hints at strong overseas sales.

If you are uncertain who might be interested in a particular subject, you might try talking with the manager of the largest new bookstore in your area. Ask the person who he or she thinks might be interested. Also in what sections might the book be positioned and why. Should you live in a small town, drive to the nearest big city to talk with the bookstore owners. Call ahead for an appointment and plan to see them during a time other than their busy period (usually midafternoon on a weekday is best). While you may get help through a telephone call, I have found that they are more cooperative in person.

Provide your background only where it is applicable. For example, suppose you are an individual with no academic training who works in a blue-collar profession. You have been interested in writing a biography, have no credentials whatever, yet are certain that you have developed your skills to the point where you can achieve your goal. Say as little about yourself as possible.

For example, my method would be to have one sentence in my cover letter which reads: "I am a Cleveland-based professional writer. This is my first biography."

The reason for mentioning your city is logical. The reason for saying "based" is more subtle. I have found that, to many editors, stating that I am "based" implies that I travel constantly. Although that is a reality for me today, I found that when I worked strictly from home, letting long-distance telephone calls serve as the extent of my traveling, I was often told that I had received an assignment because I appeared to be more versatile than other writers interested in the topic. The editors actually stressed that the other writers worked from home while I was based in Cleveland and obviously traveled all the time. Not that they wanted me to travel. They invariably told me that I could work by telephone "for this one." But I somehow came across as more sophisticated. It sounds crazy but it works.

The reason for saying you are a "professional" writer is because, by trying to sell your work, that is what you are. You don't have to have earned a specific dollar amount to be a professional. You don't have to have sold anything. But saying anything else may hurt you.

As an aside, the word "amateur" refers to someone who does something for the love of it. After well over sixty books, I am definitely an "amateur" writer in the true sense of the word. This work is simply too exhausting to write professionally if you do not love staring at blank paper (or a blank monitor) day after day, knowing you will eat only if you effectively fill it with words.

The fact that you do have a strong academic background may mean little when selling your book. Suppose you have a Ph D. in mathematics but have written a book on a silent movie star of 1923. Obviously your academic training did not prepare you for such an endeavor. I would stay with the same comments a writer should use with no background, though I would use the Ph D. with my typed signature just below my handwritten one.

Should you have a background that relates to your subject, or if you are an established writer, then you might mention it. This should still be done with subtlety, such as saying: "I am a professional writer for a number of newspapers [or magazines or periodicals]. This is my first book." Or "I am a professional writer, the author of several nonfiction books." Or "I am a music teacher for the Harper Valley School System, a background that has helped with my research into the life of Beethoven." Keep it appropriate and keep it simple, but use it if it seems that it will make a favorable impression.

Remember to always keep in mind that the less said in any cover letter, the more your work will speak for itself. I usually give no background on myself until the last page of the proposal, keeping it simple even there. My reasoning is that if the editor has read that far and liked what he or she has seen, there is no reason to reject me. On the other hand, if the editor has not liked what I have written, the fact that I have a dozen best sellers to my credit is not going to mean anything.

So what type of cover letter do I use under those circumstances? While it will vary with the book, usually it is as simple as: "Enclosed is a proposal for a biography of Count Folke Bernadotte, a Swedish diplomat responsible for saving more than thirty thousand lives during World War II. I look forward to your consideration.

"Thank you for your time and trouble.

"Sincerely . . ."

My background is included on the last page of the proposal. That way my work, and not a letter I might accidentally "screw up," does the selling.

Many new writers are rejected with their work unread because they try to say more than they should. They will say things such as: "I'm just a beginner so this may not be quite right, but I want to learn and I want to sell my book, and I'd be thrilled if you'd just tell me whatever changes you want me to make in order for you to take it." Or, "If you don't want my book, could you tell me where to send it? I'd really appreciate the help." Or, "I know it might not be good enough, but perhaps you could suggest a best-selling writer I could work with as a team so you'd want to take it." Or, "If you can't take it, I'd be happy to pay you to show me how to improve it so I don't get rejected the next time." Or, "I know this is a little slow for the first seven hundred pages, but after that I think you'll find that it just zips along." (No, I'm not making these up. These are the more common statements new writers have made, according to the editors with whom I have talked. And the statement about seven hundred dull pages was actually made directly to me at a writer's conference where a woman had the largest manuscript I had ever seen that she was certain I could sell for her.)

Keep in mind that the editor is not a writing instructor.

The editor does not want to hear self-deprecating statements like, "Although I'm nobody, after you discover me and my book becomes a best seller, I'll be famous."

The editor does not want to hear that other books on the publisher's list are "garbage" but that yours is of high literary value (another comment on the cover letter supplied by the same woman who had a manuscript that "zipped along" after the first seven hundred pages).

The editor does not want to help you sell your book.

The editor does not want to know your family history, nor does the editor want to hear that the book was tested on friends and neighbors who found it riveting.

The editor does not want to be your mentor or your friend. Let your proposal speak for itself, just the way the book must do when it is completed.

Sample Chapters

It is not necessary to send sample chapters with your proposal. Often you will not be able to truly research the material to enough of a degree to write anything without the advance. However, if you have never sold any book before, the more of the writing you can provide, the easier it will be to sell the book.

My personal feeling is that no matter how much material a publisher claims to desire, the minimum length should be approximately the first fifty pages of the book. The reason for this is that most editors have told me that they are convinced that no biographer can sustain the reader's interest for fifty pages. If the writer is determined but not very competent, he or she might be able to write ten or fifteen or even twenty-five pages that are excellent. This occurs just by the person having the drive to go over the work again and again. However, somewhere by around page 35 or 40 the burden of writing takes its toll. The quality rapidly diminishes and, by page 50, a bad work is obvious. It is boring and tedious.

The publisher likes to see as much writing as possible only to get a feel for how quickly you may be able to deliver the work. Ideally the publisher would like a completed manuscript as your first submission. However, that seldom occurs and is rarely demanded. Instead, send the proposal and, if you can, the first fifty pages or more. (Note: A thorough, well-written proposal without any material is still readily salable. Such a proposal will still give the editor a sense of your writing style.)

Mailing

As with any correspondence, you should always send an appropriately sized self-addressed, stamped envelope (SASE) for the manuscript's return. I say appropriately sized because many writers need a 10-by-13-inch envelope for sending it off, then use a 9-by-12-inch envelope for the return. They do not think they will need an equally large envelope (folded in half and inserted in the original mailing) for the return.

Also, be certain to check with the post office concerning postage. The cost of mailing is both greater and less than you may realize. Many manuscripts fit into the Priority Mail category that is quite inexpensive for excellent service.

You can send your work Special Fourth-Class Book Rate for the greatest savings. At this rate, the post office has up to six weeks to deliver your manuscript under the postal laws. However, I have found that Special Fourth-Class book manuscripts travel with the same speed as First-Class mail except during the Christmas holiday rush that starts just before Thanksgiving. During that period I always send my work either First-Class or Priority Mail, depending upon the weight.

Marketing Approach

1. Decide upon your subject.
2. Determine the sources for information concerning your subject. Make a list of your interview needs where appropriate. Determine the location of resource centers, both local and national, you will need to visit in order to produce the book.
3. Do enough research to write your proposal. This may or may not include sample chapters. If sample chapters are included, be certain to start with page 1 of the book and prepare at least the first fifty pages for the editor.
4. Write a simple cover letter. Remember, the less said with your cover letter, the better.
5. Research current biographies available for sale and see who is publishing the type you are writing. If you are researching for a children's book, be certain that you know for which age group your book is targeted. When in doubt, talk with a children's librarian at your public library or in the different school libraries (elementary, junior high, and high school). Also check the current *Writer's Market* as well as the special issues of *Publishers Weekly*. Then obtain an editor's name through the market guides, direct contact, or the current *Literary Market Place*.
6. Personalize the heading for your cover letter and prepare as many copies of your proposal as you wish to send at once.

Generally three or four sent to appropriate markets will be more than sufficient.

7. Send the book with an appropriately sized self-addressed stamped envelope (SASE) for the return. If you feel it is cheaper to make new copies rather than have the book returned, include a #10 SASE so the editor can write to you with a response.

8. Should your book be rejected, send it out again. If you have three or four copies circulating at any given time, sending out a new proposal should you be rejected by one of the companies will keep your hopes up. However, always be certain to see if the rejection is personalized in any way. If it is, notice the criticism and reread your presentation in light of the comments made and the knowledge you have gained reading this book. Rewrite where you feel such an action is appropriate. Send it out again without change where you feel a rewrite is unnecessary.

ELEVEN

Understanding the Contract

I t finally happens. You sell your book to a publisher.
Perhaps you have an agent. Perhaps you are seeking one to represent you with the final negotiations. Perhaps you are handling the contract on your own. Whatever the case, you want to be certain that you are getting a fair deal.

This chapter will not cover all the points you may face but it will give you enough background so you will understand the most critical areas. The most complete guide to reading a contract with which I am familiar is prepared by the Author's Guild. New members were provided with the contract without charge when I joined several years ago. However, the requirements for joining are strict and can only be met by selling, professional writers. As a result, the Guild will provide you with a copy of the information on understanding a contract only when you have a publisher interested in your book and a contract on the way. No matter how large or small the contract, this step makes you eligible for their Associate status and requires you send the membership fee, currently ninety dollars a year. Since you will not need the contract information until such time as you have the contract in hand, this will be the least expensive way to gain the information you need. Contact the Authors Guild, Inc., at 234 West 44th Street, New York, NY 10036.

Money

Let's start the discussion of your contract with the issue of money. This is a far greater concern for most authors than completion dates or other technicalities. How much can you expect for an advance? On what is the advance offer based? And do you ever have to return advance money?

The advance is determined by the number of books a company expects to sell in a relatively short period of time (a few weeks, a few months, or a year, depending upon the publisher). They want to pay you no more in advance than you will predictably earn from the sales of the book. To understand how this is done, you first need to know the royalty schedule.

For simplicity, let us look at a hardback book that will sell for twenty dollars in the stores. The publisher does not make twenty dollars on each book. The publisher will gross approximately half that amount when selling the book to a distributor who marks it up and sells it to the bookstore where it is then sold to the buyer. This means that ten dollars will go to the publisher and must cover all publishing costs, including a royalty for the author, as well as any profit that will be made. The remaining ten dollars must cover the profit to be made by both the distributor and the retailer.

The royalties for hardback books will vary, though most publishers offer ten percent of what they charge the distributor (often called "publisher's net") for the first five thousand copies sold, 12½ percent of the next five thousand, and 15 percent for copies in excess of the first ten thousand. There are other ways some publishers work, but the figures provided are fairly standard in the industry.

Looking at this on a practical basis, if the cover price is twenty dollars, the publisher's net will be ten dollars (in reality, the publisher's net may be anywhere from 40 percent to 60 percent of the cover price. This example was selected because it is easy to understand). Your 10 percent royalty for each of the first five thousand copies will be $1 per book. The second five thousand copies will earn you $1.25 per book. And the copies in excess of ten thousand will earn you $1.50 per book.

Now comes what the publishers call the "number crunching." How many books can they expect to sell in a limited amount of time? If the minimum expectation is 3,500 copies, then you will be offered no more than $3,500 as an advance. On the other hand if the minimum expectation is 50,000 copies, then you might be offered from $50,000 to $75,000 as your advance.

There is no minimum a publisher might offer you. However, there is a maximum figure beyond which a publisher will not go based on the formula I have given you.

The advance will be offered in one of four ways. Most publishers will offer you half the money upon signing and half upon the satisfactory completion of the manuscript. Other publishers will offer you a portion upon signing (one fourth or one third), a portion halfway through the manuscript (either the second one fourth or one third), and the remainder upon satisfactory completion (either the last half or the remaining third) of the manuscript.

A significantly smaller number of publishers will ask you to write the book without an up-front advance because you have never written before. Then they will pay the advance upon satisfactory completion of the manuscript. And the rest, a very tiny number of publishers, will pay the advance upon publication—a time that might be as long as one-and-a-half years or more after you obtain the contract to write the book.

The royalties begin accumulating with your first sale. These are credited against your advance. When the royalties exceed the advance, you begin getting checks, usually every six months. Should the royalties be equal to or less than what was paid for your advance, you will never receive another cent. However, you never have to repay the publisher if the book does not earn back the advance. So long as you have satisfactorily completed the book manuscript, a situation that exists usually when the final advance check is issued and/or a letter is sent telling you that the book and any expected rewrite is fine, you owe the publisher nothing.

Expenses

It is rare that an author receives additional money for expenses. There was a time when authors assumed that the advance was meant to provide them with the money needed for living while writing the book. This would mean paying for housing, food, telephone, and travel, at the very least. That was seldom the case for most writers and is certainly not normal today. Advances are based on predicted sales. If those predictable sales are high enough, all expenses are probably going to be met through the advance just because the offer will be large. If the predictable sales do not warrant that much money, the lack of funds becomes your problem. In both cases, the payment of expenses is highly unlikely.

There are some exceptions to the no-expenses rule that you can demand. For example, I agreed to write a book that will require extensive time spent in Manhattan, one of the most expensive cities in the United States when seeking hotel space. My work will require a slightly larger room than some of the less expensive hotels maintain because I will be traveling with a laptop computer and working in my room. Yet none of my travel costs will be met by the publisher.

In addition to the travel, the publisher wants me to find photographs to illustrate the book. There will be a fee charged by the estate of the subject about whom I am writing and this would normally further deplete my advance money. I explained to the publisher that I thought it was unrealistic to expect me to meet those expenses out of my advance. The publisher agreed and gave me a maximum picture-buying budget to cover the additional costs.

This circumstance is true for many publishers. If you are expected to meet certain expenses out of pocket, and if these have nothing to do with normal travel, photocopying of documents, or related matters, additional funds may be made available to you. But the cost of travel, hotels, and so forth generally are considered to be a part of what you must pay from your advance.

Work for Hire

The one exception to the expenses procedure may come with work-for-hire arrangements. Under work for hire, you, the author, receive a flat fee under contract to write a book. You do not share in the copyright, which usually goes to the person who hired you. And you do not share in the royalties the book will earn. (There are exceptions, of course. Some work-for-hire arrangements have a flat fee plus a percentage of the royalties, though that percentage may be quite small or payable only after a certain number of copies, often in excess of the number needed to return the advance, are sold.)

Work-for-hire arrangements are probably most common for true ghostwriters. Many of the books for which I ghost have my name in the copyright notice so that I can open the book and show the fine print to a publisher who wants to know my credits. But occasionally the subject's ego is such that he or she wants no credit given to the true writer and wants to take all of the money earned. An agreement is reached where the writer produces the book for a set fee.

Sometimes the ghosted book is then self-published by a vanity press or small press operation, the writer usually making the most money since such publishing is rarely profitable. At other times the ghosted book is published by a major publisher and has the potential for great success. One psychologist for whom I ghost has gone both the small press route and also with publishing giant Simon & Schuster. The latter had excellent distribution. The former eventually had sales only through two outlets.

Collaboration Agreements

The arrangements you make when working with someone, either a coresearcher or the subject of an as-told-to autobiography, is usually not the concern of the publisher. There are occasions when the publisher will make the connection of a writer and subject. I worked that way on the DeLorean book, having been hired by the publisher, with the approval of John DeLorean, and paid by the publisher. The agreement was work for hire and I was given an expense account to cover hotel, travel, food, and any unusual telephone calls. I did not share in the royalties in any way, though the book went on to become a best seller.

By contrast, I normally work for an equal share of the money. My reasoning is that the subject has a story to tell that cannot be told without the assistance of a writer. At the same time, I have all the writing skills but cannot produce a book without access to a good story. Each of us is bringing an equal skill to all this and thus we should be paid equally.

Determining the Split

There is no proper way to divide money when working on an as-told-to book. True collaborators on a biography, both researching though usually only one doing the final writing in order for the book to have one "voice," generally split the gross on a fifty-fifty basis. The as-told-to collaborator is different, though, because you are frequently working with a celebrity or at least someone in the news. That person may have large sums of money or a major book advance potential. Or that person may have great fame but no money at all, barely surviving and feeling that he or she deserves the bulk of the money.

I cannot give you an approach you should use. What I will do is tell you the different ways in which authors work so you can decide for yourself what is best.

The straight fee basis: A work-for-hire arrangement is a risk for both subject and writer. The subject risks the book not doing so well as anticipated and thus making nothing or very little from a book he or she perhaps expected to make large sums of money.

By contrast, the writer risks receiving a small sum of money while the subject gets very rich. For example, the original arrangement for *Iacocca* provided William Novak with $45,000 to write the book from tapes provided by Lee Iacocca. While a few thousand dollars' bonus was eventually added, the book was a major best seller earning Iacocca millions of dollars.

Sometimes the writer becomes jealous of the book's success (Novak did not, though he has not worked on a strictly work-for-hire arrangement since) and is embittered by the experience. At other times the subject feels he or she was "taken" by the writer when the truth was that the subject had been unwilling to make what would have been a far more equitable split. Even worse, the subject may fear that the writer will never give 100 percent of his or her ability because of the work-for-hire arrangement, telling others that the writer cheated the subject if the book does not do well. This risk is compounded if the writer is successful because the expectations of the subject become greater.

For example, I once had someone approach me and say, "I want you to write my autobiography. I know it's not really that interesting, but you've been so successful, with your name attached, I know we'll get rich." Naturally I refused to work with the person. I have also refused to work with someone essentially making the same request and statement who was also rather famous. The expectations of the subject were not likely to be met and I had obviously been set up to be the "fall guy."

The fifty-fifty split: I believe in fifty-fifty splits, something with which many other writers disagree. The subject and I take half the money. If the book succeeds, we share equally. If it bombs, we suffer equally. There is no chance for jealousy. There is no chance for me to be accused of giving less than my best because I am going to be financially hurt if I do.

There are two common complaints to the fifty-fifty split. One was raised by the widow of a famous comedian who died broke. She essentially said, "You're nothing without my story. I lived with him for years. I nursed him through his drug habits. I was with him in the good times and the bad. Now I'm broke and you want to take half the money? Forget it. I'll find someone who will work for less."

The second complaint comes from the individual who will predictably receive a major advance in the high six figures or greater. If Elizabeth Taylor or Senator Ted Kennedy were to agree to write no-holds-barred autobiographies, the bidding would start at a million dollars each and probably go higher. There is no reason why they should pay a writer a half-million dollars or more up front, though I'd be happy to take it if I were the one called to do the writing. More likely they would offer their collaborators a set fee of perhaps $100,000 or more to handle the writing. They might also offer either a tiny percentage of royalties or a fifty-fifty split of the money to be made after the advance was paid back through royalty earnings.

Advance fees to author, royalties split fifty-fifty: One of the more common ways in which collaborators work is by the author taking the entire advance, the author and subject splitting all royalties on a fifty-fifty basis. This presents a problem for the subject, though, because the total income from the project may not exceed the advance. This is certainly the case with the vast majority of books sold in the United States.

The reasoning makes sense with this arrangement. Advance money is often fairly low. The writer often has to travel to the subject, may have to meet tape transcription fees out of pocket, and have other expenses up front. The writer also has to survive financially while the book is being written and may have no other source of income. For example, in one instance of which I am aware, the advance paid for a book was $8,000 and the author had to spend extensive time flying back and forth to a small California community. However, the subject worked as a checkout clerk in a supermarket and needed to have open heart surgery. The timing for the book and the predictability of the sales were such that it might be two to three years after signing the contract that she would receive any money. Had she obtained the $3,600 ($4,000 less a 10 percent agent's fee — the agent's fee is always off the top when the advance is paid, and an agent was used for this book), she could have afforded the difference between what her insurance paid and the cost of the needed operation, improving her health. As it was, she was literally at risk of dying before she had a chance to see any money. The circumstances are extreme but they do illustrate the problem with this type of agreement, even though the argument in favor of the author's needs is valid.

Work for hire plus a percentage: A less common approach, but one that some writers prefer, is to have a work-for-hire agreement plus a percentage of the gross either before or after the advance is paid back. This can be any way the collaborators decide. The subject might pay the writer a flat fee, then 10 percent of the royalties. Or the writer might get a flat fee, nothing more until the advance is paid back, and then 50 percent of everything that is earned from then on. Or some other, mutually satisfactory arrangement is made.

Expenses: All of the methods for splitting fees involve expenses. At the very least you will have to pay for recording tapes, transcriptions, and the time spent writing. You may also have to travel and use long-distance telephone calls. The latter are quite high and, even with a discount service, my bills while interviewing usually start at six hundred dollars per month and have gone much higher.

Expenses can also be padded. For example, when I fly from my home in Cleveland to Los Angeles, do I fly first class or coach? Do I make my reservations more than two weeks in advance to take advantage of special fares or do I fly with shorter notice for a much higher charge? If I need a rental car, do I get the least expensive subcompact from an off-airport location or do I stroll up to the Hertz counter and ask for something glamorous? Do I take the least expensive, clean, safe hotel I can find or do I go for the comfort of a top-of-the-line hotel, perhaps with an oversized room? Do I eat in the hotel restaurants, including ordering from room service when I want to work late, or do I walk across the street to a more moderately priced location?

Notice how all of my expenses can be justified whichever choice I make. I fly coach because I am 5'9" tall, not obese, and can use the fold-down tray to hold my computer so I can work as I fly. Or I could fly first class because I need to land perfectly refreshed and the extra room causes less tension than the crowded cabin seats. And I could make my reservations for the next day since I am a busy man, very much in demand, and want to make certain nothing pressing comes along. Yet the difference per flight might be six hundred to one thousand dollars or more, depending upon the season.

It is so easy to justify expenses, I worry about cheating my subject. Taking all expenses off the top seems fair until you realize how easy it is to exaggerate "necessities." My preference is for each of us to pay our expenses out of our share of the money. If I choose to fly across country to meet with someone, that is my problem. If the person wants to come to see me, then he or she will pay that bill. Generally this means that the bulk of the expenses are my own, a futher reason why I am comfortable with the fifty-fifty split of the gross. The only expense shared equally is the agent's commission, if any. I insist that the agent's commission is taken off the top. If the advance is $10,000, then the agent takes $1,000 and splits the remaining $9,000 equally between the subject and me.

In the case of the comedian's widow, for example, she was irate that I would take half of "her" advance. I would have had to fly to Hawaii to work with her and call her in that island state to follow up on our work. I would have had unusually high hotel bills because we would have been working during the tourist season when costs are greater than normal. And I still would have had the transcriptions and other concerns. My ultimate share of the advance money would have been extremely low once my expenses were removed. Yet she refused to consider these facts and there was nothing I could do to convince her otherwise.

The problem we face as writers is that we cannot ignore the finanacial realities of a project just because we want to do it. The idea of working with someone who is fascinating, perhaps glamorous, and regularly in the news is so exciting that there is a tendency to want to agree to any arrangement demanded. Yet we still must do the work. We still must pay for travel, telephone calls, photocopying, tape recording, and all the other expenses. There is a point where we have to say "no" and pity the writer who yields to the temptation to do the work for less than should be asked.

Contracting Payments

There are several ways you can be paid by the publisher. If you use an agent, it is traditional for the publisher to pay the agent and the agent to divide the money as designated. This means that if you are splitting the fees on a fifty-fifty basis, the agent will take his or her percentage off the top, then divide the money equally, sending each of you a separate check.

On occasion a different arrangement is worked out. This usually occurs when the writer or subject is uneasy about having the agent receive the money. Then three checks are issued. One goes to the agent, the remainder being split between the collaborators.

When no agent is used, checks should be sent directly from the publisher to each of the coauthors in the percentages arranged between the collaborators. This prevents either party from taking more than an agreed-upon share. Likewise if there are problems collecting the money, the publisher becomes the bad guy, not either collaborator. My attitude is that I want each person with whom I work to be interested in working with me on a future book. This will happen so long as everyone acts fairly and neither collaborator feels that the other has a way of cheating.

Collaboration Agreement

A collaboration agreement is an agreement between the writers concerning how the money will be divided. It is written and signed before the contract is arranged with the publisher. Its purpose is to protect everyone involved with the project. It is also a waste of time.

The truth about collaboration is that it will work or it won't. If you and the subject work to the point of a successful proposal, then the subject decides to write alone or work with someone else before you are both under a publishing contract, there is nothing that you can do about it. You have wasted the time necessary for preliminary interviews. You have wasted the time needed to write the proposal. But you have not wasted the time you might spend fighting over a contract with someone who is dishonest, dishonorable, and/or simply doesn't want to work with you.

My tendency is to forget the collaboration agreement and let the publisher's contract spell out the rights and obligations of you and your subject. (If you are working alone, such as with a historical biography or an unauthorized biography, there will be no collaboration agreement.) However, there are two good reasons to arrange for such an agreement. One is because you are working with someone who is uncertain about you and the book writing, who needs an agreement to be comfortable. The other is because you will be dealing with confidential materials or information that should not be made public before the book is published.

When these instances arise, I usually write my own agreement. The following is a sample I have used. Remember that the arrangement is only until the book is under contract with the publisher. Then the contract with the publisher takes precedence.

> This is an agreement between (Author) and (name of Subject). It is understood that (Author) and (Subject) will work together on a book on (the Subject's) life. Toward this end, (Subject) will make him/her self available for interviews in person and by telephone, will supply all documents and other papers, and will assist with locating additional people to interview if necessary. (Author) will use all this information in order to prepare a book proposal for sale to major publishers. Toward this end, (Author) and (Subject) will split all income on a fifty-fifty basis, less (percentage) of the gross given to the agent if an agent is used.
>
> It is understood that (Author) will be provided information that is confidential in nature. (Author) will not use this material for other articles, books, or any other purpose without written permission from (Subject). Likewise, (Subject) will not work with any other author to prepare an identical book while this proposal is being sold. However, (Subject) may work with a different author for any noncompeting project related to book publishing, newspapers, magazines, radio, or film.
>
> Should the book fail to sell, or should there be a decision in writing to not continue with this partnership, all confidential materials supplied to (Author) by (Subject) will be returned.

This type of agreement assures the commitment of your subject while not causing your subject to worry about the possibility of your "stealing" confidential information. It also stresses the subject's right to work with someone else, though not on competing materials at the time you are trying to sell your book. I often will also add the line: "This agreement will be superseded by any contract with a publisher."

Royalty Payments

Royalty payments may be made quarterly, annually, or every six months. Most companies work on a six-month basis, but they pay on a timetable that allows them to hold your money for three months after it has been collected. Typically you will be told that you will earn money from January 1 through June 30, the money to be paid in October. Your check for July 1 through December 31 will be sent in March or April. There may also be a small percentage, never more than 20 percent, withheld from your pay in any six-month period to cover returns by the bookstores.

All companies have a minimum amount of money, usually more than twenty-five dollars, that a book has to earn in a given six-month period before you will be sent a check. If it earns less than that, the checks are generally issued annually.

Subrights

Subrights is a term that covers sales other than the initial sale of your biography. A First Serial Rights sale means that a publication has purchased the right to be the first magazine or newspaper to publish an excerpt from your book. This is a section quoted exactly as it will appear in the book, the excerpt usually appearing at the same time that the book is released in the stores.

Publishers will make two considerations when offering First Serial Rights. One is who will pay the most money. The other is in which publication will the appearance result in the greatest number of sales. Book publishers seldom, if ever, look to see which publication will supply the greatest prestige.

For example, when the Peter Lawford biography was offered for First Serial Rights, the two highest bidders were *Cosmopolitan* and the *National Enquirer*. We agreed to have the *Enquirer* buy it, a choice that led many friends to ask how we could do such a thing. The *Enquirer* had no "class," according to them. There was no prestige. It was embarrassing to even see it at the checkout counter, they complained. But the *Enquirer* offered almost six times the money of the more "prestigious" *Cosmopolitan*, the latter preferring to save its bigger money offers for original articles done for the magazine.

At other times the First Serial Rights might be sold to a magazine that has a limited circulation, a relatively low rate of pay, but whose readers are likely to be among the primary buyers for the book you have written. Remember that the publisher wants to sell as many books as possible so the decisions made will almost always work in your favor.

There are other rights sold. There may be Second Serial Rights which allows a publication to be the second one to quote an excerpt. There are paperback rights, sales to book clubs, overseas sales, and even articles written about the same topic where you may share in the money. Movie rights are also a possibility, a subject discussed later.

The publisher will always want to share in the subrights income from your book. Usually the contract will be a form that lists the share the publisher will take, implying that it is etched in stone. However, all subrights are negotiable.

As a general rule, the least the writer should expect is 50 percent of the subrights income. This is identical whether you are working alone or collaborating with someone.

The most you should expect is 90 percent, the remaining 10 percent going to the publisher. Generally you can negotiate between 65 percent and 90 percent for yourself for each area.

The publisher will be most demanding about sharing in the subrights income if the book is somewhat of a gamble when it comes to sales potential. The money from the sale of subrights often offsets financial problems that otherwise might exist. For example, when the book *Sybil* was published in hardback several years ago, it became what was seemingly an overnight best seller. More and more books were rushed into print at considerable cost. Unfortunately the publisher overestimated the demand for hardbacks to the point where, almost as quickly as the book had been selling, the sales stopped. Thousands of hardbacks were returned. The waste was so great that, instead of making massive profits as would have been the case with equal sales but fewer remainders, the publishing company was likely to lose money. Fortunately the book sold to a paperback house for a considerable sum and the share of those subrights that went to the publisher made the book profitable. Had that not occurred, the company would have had financial trouble.

In other instances the hardback does quite poorly but the paperback does well, there is a movie sale, or some other situation occurs that compensates for the problems created when sales and print runs are badly at variance. Thus there will always be a desire by the publisher to take as much of the extra money related to the project as they can negotiate. However, negotiate is the key word and there will be a certain amount of flexibility in their minimum demands. This is where some writers feel an agent is their best protection, though as mentioned earlier, when you get to the stage where you are talking contract, almost any agent will represent you, at least for that project.

Free Copies

The number of free copies you receive of your book will vary with the publisher. This is a minor point but it becomes major to authors who want to give them away to every friend, acquaintance, and former schoolteacher who said they would never amount to anything. Even worse, writers' demands for free books can be a source of extreme annoyance for the publishers.

The book is the publisher's product, just as shoes are the product of the shoemaker and stereos are the product of an electronics company. You will generally be provided with no more than a dozen copies of your own book. Anything more you will be allowed to purchase at the discount given to the distributors, usually 40 percent off or a little more. This is extremely fair, especially since some writers like to sell their books at writers' conferences and courses they teach, charging full retail or close to full retail, taking money away from area bookstores whose owners form the lifeblood of retail publishing. When the author receives a discount, he or she has the option, in effect, of being another distributor. You still make a royalty and the publisher loses no money.

Other Forms of Reproduction

Do not ignore the clauses that talk about electronic reproduction of your book. Increasing numbers of books are being reproduced in ways other than print. In the past few years I have seen my books appearing on audiocassette for the average listener, not just the visually impaired. I have also had companies ask me about the possibility of one of my books being placed on computer disk for reading on a monitor. Video disks (essentially a larger version of a compact music disk but designed to reproduce feature films, books, and photographs) and videotape uses are becoming more involved than in the past. Within the predictable life of your book, there may come a point where it is desired for electronic reproduction. You should retain the largest possible percentage of these rights when negotiating.

Other Points

Be certain the book is copyrighted in your name by the publisher. You do not have to copyright your own book. The publisher will do this for you, giving you the ownership for the remainder of your life plus fifty years. Either it will be meaningless by the time that you die or a potentially substantial legacy for your heirs.

Make yourself available for any promotion. Many books are not promoted. This sounds foolish but is the reality of publishing. When they are promoted, few authors receive the grand tour of shows ranging from Oprah Winfrey to Johnny Carson. More likely you will be handling call-in radio shows and taped programs from your home. You may also appear regionally.

There is no pay for making appearances. Expenses are strictly controlled and the time involvement is relatively great. However, it is important that you cooperate fully. When you are interviewed, you must act as an entertainer, delighting your listener with the most interesting stories from your book. Don't try to sell your book. Don't cut a story short, telling listeners that if they want to know what happened, they will have to read your book. Instead, give your best material because most listeners are certain you are holding back something even better. If they like you and the stories you tell, they will want to read what you have written.

Movie options are fairly common for many books. An option is a fee a production company pays for the right to make a film from the book. No one else may buy the rights during the period when the option is in effect — usually from six months to one year with a possible renewal. It is rare for a book to actually be made into a movie, though. It has been estimated that for every fifty options sold in Hollywood, one will go into development far enough for a script to be written. And for every three development projects that go to script, one will actually get aired on television, in theaters, or as an original videotape.

The fact that your book is sold to Hollywood does not mean that you will be asked to write the script. Some writers do not want to do this. Some writers currently lack the skills. And some writers have no trouble learning the form but are not desired by the production companies because they have other commitments.

Even when you do become involved with the writing, there are three ways this might occur. One is where you write the treatment. This is simply the story told from beginning to end. It can be as short as a couple of paragraphs or as long as twenty-five or thirty pages. Generally the shorter the better, though the minimum pay required by the Writer's Guild of America, West, for all writers, regardless of whether or not they are as yet members of the union, is extremely high.

Next comes the first-draft screenplay. The union breaks script payments for most writers into first and second drafts. Unlike other fields, though, a first draft is actually a finished product. As with any writing that you do, you work your heart and soul out, then turn in the best of which you are capable. However, should it not be good enough, or should the company have another writer under contract who has been guaranteed a certain number of projects per year, a second draft is done. Sometimes this improves the script. Sometimes this is just a way of paying off another writer. In either case, a separate fee is paid. Hopefully you will get both, though as a new person in this field, you will usually be lucky just to get one.

No matter what, your option will be paid against an ultimate fee to be paid at the time of production. For example, suppose you get a $5,000 option for one year. This might be against a $50,000 total purchase price to be paid the day filming starts. The option money is usually subtracted from the total fee owed so you get $5,000 up front and the $45,000 when filming starts. Fees for treatments, scripts, or anything else are always additional. There may also be bonuses if the book is unusually successful, such as making the *New York Times* Best Seller List.

To sell your work in Hollywood you will need an agent. Unlike book publishing, Hollywood agents are easy to obtain and serve a less-than-useful purpose in most cases.

Hollywood is a union town where labor is sharply divided. Every aspect of the movie business has a union involved. Sometimes there is much "make work," such as with the submission of material. Most agents act as conduits, doing nothing that you could not do yourself. Yet you must use them.

In order to sell your work, there are two steps to take. First, contact Writers Guild of America, West, 8955 Beverly Blvd., West Hollywood, CA 90048 (213-550-1000) and ask for their list of approved agents. You will be expected to send a fee of a dollar or two, plus a self-addressed, stamped #10 business envelope in order to receive their list of approved agents. These are all agents who are signatories to the Writers Guild minimum contract agreement.

When you look at the agent list, you will notice that approximately two-thirds have asterisks by their names. This means that they will look at the work of new writers. Call a few of these companies, explain that you have a published book on whatever subject you have written about, and that you would like to see if they feel it can be sold to the film industry. Send the book to whichever agents are interested (most will be interested in a book though they will not be interested in the same idea before it has sold to a book company). One of them will represent the project if it seems to be marketable to the film industry.

The commission charged will be either 10 percent or 15 percent, depending upon the agent. This is charged against the movie sale. The Hollywood agent selling film rights does not receive a portion of the book money. Likewise, the book agent, if any is used, usually does not receive any of the screen money. The one crossover exception occurs when a book agent also has a Hollywood agent connection, in which case that one agency handles everything for a fee of 10 percent to 15 percent of everything sold.

Film rights may or may not have to be shared with the book publisher. Either way, be certain a film project is pursued by either you, your publisher, or your book agent if one is used. Your book will probably not become a movie, but it can bring you a check for option money, a nice bonus.

Attorneys

Most attorneys will tell you that you should always have a lawyer check your contract to be certain it is legal. What they don't say is that few attorneys have ever seen book contracts and certainly do not know what is standard and what is negotiable. Some will research this field on your behalf, naturally charging for the time. Others will decide that a contract is a contract and act as though the blind are leading the blind. Either way you have a contract.

My feeling is that if you cannot understand the contract you receive, you should not sign it. Use the Authors Guild information packet on contracts. Read the material carefully and ask for clarification of the parts you do not understand. It is perfectly fair to rewrite any confusing section as agreed upon and replace the printed section with the rewrite, both parties agreeing to the statement.

If you still are unsure, you might contact an agent since you will have a book contract and the time spent by the agent will be so minimal that it is worth the 10 percent of even a small advance. Should you wish to use an attorney, rely only on those with a good history of handling book contracts. My tendency would be to rely upon referrals from the Authors Guild and from editorial people in publishing companies. I would not rely upon Bar Association referral lists, especially if you are living outside major publishing centers.

TWELVE

Afterword

Now that you understand the marketplace, it is time to start your biography. This will be one of the most exciting adventures you can have. You become an investigative reporter, an empathetic friend, a voyeur, a busybody, gossip, historian, and chronicler, all in one. You will come to know a life and a period of time more intimately than anyone other than your subject. And you will be challenged in the writing to make that life come alive in a manner that will enable your reader to share his or her world almost as completely as your subject lived it.

Also remember that no matter how much fun you have, and this is one of the most delightful forms of nonfiction writing you will encounter, always think of your reader. Write for the enjoyment of the person who has yet to encounter the world you are researching and your book will be successful. This is very much a giving profession yet one from which you will derive extensive pleasure, at least a modest income, and the possibility of great success.

Now go to work and let me hear how you are doing. Feel free to write in care of the publisher. I am rooting for your success and would be pleased to know that you have been helped along the way.

INDEX

Other Books of Interest

Manuscript Submission, by Scott Edelstein $13.95
Plot, by Ansen Dibell $13.95
Revision, by Kit Reed $13.95
Spider Spin Me a Web: Lawrence Block on Writing Fiction, by Lawrence Block $16.95
Storycrafting, by Paul Darcy Boles (paper) $10.95
Theme & Strategy, by Ronald B. Tobias $13.95
Writing the Novel: From Plot to Print, by Lawrence Block (paper) $10.95

Special Interest Writing Books

The Children's Picture Book: How to Write It, How to Sell It, by Ellen E.M. Roberts (paper) $16.95
Comedy Writing Secrets, by Melvin Helitzer $18.95
The Complete Book of Scriptwriting, by J. Michael Straczynski (paper) $11.95
Editing Your Newsletter, by Mark Beach (paper) $18.50
Families Writing, by Peter Stillman $15.95
How to Write a Play, by Raymond Hull (paper) $12.95
How to Write Action/Adventure Novels, by Michael Newton $13.95
How to Write & Sell A Column, by Raskin & Males $10.95
How to Write and Sell Your Personal Experiences, by Lois Duncan (paper) $10.95
How to Write Mysteries, by Shannon OCork $13.95
How to Write Romances, by Phyllis Taylor Pianka $13.95
How to Write the Story of Your Life, by Frank P. Thomas (paper) $11.95
How to Write Western Novels, by Matt Braun $13.95
The Poet's Handbook, by Judson Jerome (paper) $10.95
Successful Lyric Writing (workbook), by Sheila Davis (paper) $16.95
Successful Scriptwriting, by Jurgen Wolff & Kerry Cox $18.95
Travel Writer's Handbook, by Louise Zobel (paper) $11.95
TV Scriptwriter's Handbook, by Alfred Brenner (paper) $10.95
Writing for Children & Teenagers, 3rd Edition, by Lee Wyndham & Arnold Madison (paper) $12.95
Writing to Inspire, edited by William Gentz (paper) $14.95

The Writing Business

A Beginner's Guide to Getting Published, edited by Kirk Polking $11.95
The Complete Guide to Self-Publishing, by Tom & Marilyn Ross (paper) $16.95
How to Sell & Re-Sell Your Writing, by Duane Newcomb $11.95
How to Write with a Collaborator, by Hal Bennett with Michael Larsen $11.95
How You Can Make $25,000 a Year Writing, by Nancy Edmonds Hanson (paper) $12.95
Is There a Speech Inside You?, by Don Aslett (paper) $9.95
Literary Agents: How to Get & Work with the Right One for You, by Michael Larsen $9.95
Professional Etiquette for Writers, by William Brohaugh $9.95
Time Management for Writers, by Ted Schwarz $10.95
The Writer's Friendly Legal Guide, edited by Kirk Polking $16.95
A Writer's Guide to Contract Negotiations, by Richard Balkin (paper) $11.95

To order directly from the publisher, include $3.00 postage and handling for 1 book and $1.00 for each additional book. Allow 30 days for delivery.

Writer's Digest Books
1507 Dana Avenue, Cincinnati, Ohio 45207
Credit card orders call TOLL-FREE
1-800-289-0963
Prices subject to change without notice.

Write to this same address for information on *Writer's Digest* magazine, Writer's Digest Book Club, Writer's Digest School, and Writer's Digest Criticism Service.